The Most ENORMOUS Book of
Nuts

A MESSAGE FROM THE NUTS EDITOR

Oh, hello! Sorry, I was distracted there, by the very book that you're holding in your hands! Yes, that's right, even the people who edit this book are transfixed by how good it is. It's *The Most Enormous Book Of Nuts* – and it really is spectacular!

From the people who brought you the record-breaking, ground-breaking, everything-breaking *Nuts* magazine, *The Most Enormous Book Of Nuts* is the follow-up to the hit *Big Book Of Nuts* and, like that fine tome, it's a crazy combination of astonishingly sexy women, astonishingly sexy cars, astonishingly astonishing weird facts and loads of top-drawer sport. It's everything you love in *Nuts*, but in book form.

Our crack team of *Nuts* types have selected our very finest moments and crammed them between two hard covers, so you can dip into this book whenever you like and be assured of immediate entertainment. This, we reckon, makes it better than anything by Shakespeare and Dickens combined. Enjoy!

Dom, Editor

Nuts CONTENTS

GIRLS

OTHER STUFF

TWICE THE FUN

SOPHIE AND SAM

To start this book off we thought we could do a lot worse than feature Nuts favourite Sophie Howard and lovely Page 3 Idol winner Sam Cooke in their first joint Nuts photo shoot. Enjoy!

Sophie, you've just felt Sam's boobs – currently the best boobs in Britain. What are they like? They're very round and very pert. They're definitely the best boobs in Britain by far.

Sam, what was it like cupping the boobs of a certified legend in your mere mortal hands? Well, I was nervous before we met but she's not nearly as intimidating as I thought. She's got fantastic big boobs and a tiny body, and she's really nice.

You two lovely ladies have been fronting *Nuts*' Girls Getting Friendly With Other Girls. So, when it comes to doing it with the fairer sex: have you, would you, could you and should you?

"My boobs are too small for melons. Possibly, they're more like grapefruits"
Sam

Sophie: I have, once. But I wouldn't any more. I could hold hands but I couldn't kiss another girl now. I like men too much.

Sam: I would, but I wouldn't really want to. Girls don't really appeal to me. I've snogged some of my mates when I was younger, but it's not as good as snogging a bloke.

Sophie: I always find girls are much sloppier. There's too much lip gloss. You kiss a girl and it's like you're getting a full face wash.

If your boobs opened a fruit and veg shop, what would they sell?

Sophie: That depends on my boobs. Maybe they'd sell cucumbers. Ha-ha!

Sam: It's a tricky one. My boobs are too small for melons. Possibly, they're more like grapefruits.

Sophie: Or a small melon. Like a honeydew, not a watermelon. If a man's ever lucky enough to have a threesome, where on earth does he start, with four boobs at once?

Sam: He'd have to take it in turns. Otherwise, they'd complain he's not giving each his full attention.

Sophie: It all depends how much everyone's into it, I suppose. Well, let's imagine some scenarios. First, a threesome where the man's tired but the two girls are up for it.

Sophie: He could lie down and one girl could sit on his face, the other on his lap.

How about if the man's up for it, one girl's tired, but the other's up for it?

Sophie: The tired girl should go missionary so she can lie down, and the more energetic girl can jiggle her boobs in his face.

What if the man's up for it but both girls are tired?

Sophie: Then the two girls should go home and watch a DVD and he'll have some time alone. Ha-ha!

Who has the biggest boobs?

Sophie: Mine are 34G.

Sam: Mine were 30F but I'm not sure at the moment. They keep going bigger and smaller.

Maybe your eyesight's going and your boobs are the same size?

Sam: Maybe it's my paranoia. I'm constantly worried about my boobs. But I still fit in my bras, so I'm still a 30F. An F-cup makes me sound like I've got huge boobs but they're not that big – it's just because I've got a small back.

All this talk of boobs and we haven't got onto your lovely bottoms yet. How about a quick marks-out-of-ten review of each other's behind?

Sam: Sophie was telling me earlier that she doesn't have a bum.

"He could lie down and one girl could sit on his face, the other on his lap"
Sophie

Sophie: I don't have a bum. I just have an extension of my thigh and my back. I need bum implants. Sam's bum is very pert, just like her top half. I'd say a good 9.9 out of ten. You better not give my bum a really low score now, Sam.

We'll give her an 8. Sophie, every time a new girl is asked who they'd love to pose with, your name is always top of the list. Does it make you feel special?

It's a real compliment. I have to admit though, every time a new girl comes out I think, "Here comes my replacement!" It's alright, it's got to happen some time I suppose.

How come you were wearing matching knickers earlier?
Sophie: We're actually psychic! We sent secret psychic messages when we were getting dressed this morning. Just kidding! We just thought they looked good today and thought, "Why not?"

And finally, will you be seeing each other again?
Sophie: I hope *Nuts* will get us together for a shoot again soon!

"Mine were 30F but I'm not sure at the moment. They keep going bigger and smaller"

Sam

11

Nuts PUBAMMO

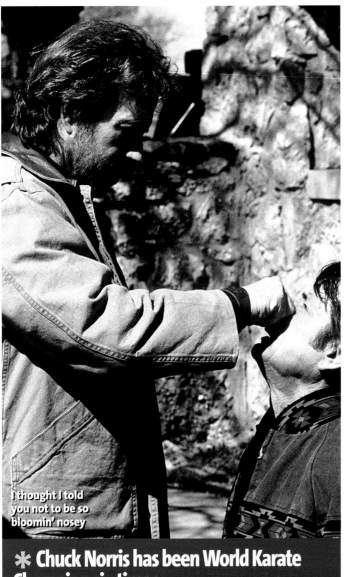

I thought I told you not to be so bloomin' nosey

✳ Chuck Norris has been World Karate Champion six times

✳ The first fiver was printed in 1793.
✳ **William Shatner**'s kidney stone was sold for $25,000 in an online auction in 2006.
✳ **100 million videos are viewed every day on YouTube.**
✳ The Swiss invented cellophane, milk chocolate and Velcro.
✳ **The Honourable Artillery Company is the oldest surviving regiment in the British Army.**
✳ **It only took Stephen King 72** hours to write *The Running Man*.
✳ **Nelson** was shot at a range of 50 feet by a French sniper.
✳ **196 million cups of tea are drunk every day in Britain.**
✳ The gap between large asteroids in an asteroid belt is two million kilometres.
✳ **Only five people died in the Great Fire of London.**
✳ 1,503 passengers were lost when the **RMS Titanic** sunk.
✳ 33 moons orbit Saturn.

✳ A falling person reaches 120mph after falling 32 storeys.
✳ Your sense of smell is 10,000 times more sensitive than your sense of taste.
✳ **Rocky Marciano retired unbeaten with a record 49 wins, 43 by KO. He is the only undefeated heavyweight champion in professional boxing history.**
✳ On average, shark attacks happen in Australian seas 15 times a year.
✳ **The release date for *Spider-Man 3* was set before *Spider-Man 2* was released.**
✳ Maggots clean wounds 18 times faster than antibiotics.
✳ **A bowling ball outweighs a ping pong ball 2,800 to one.**
✳ In 2004 alone, Russia exported £14,555,000,000 worth of arms.
✳ **A spaceship travelling at 25,000mph would take over 113,200 years to reach the Earth's closest star.**

Beth Ditto's breakfast was nearly ready

✳ Five million sausages are eaten every day in Britain

Meeow!

✳ Tiger cubs are only 40 per cent of the weight of a newborn human

✳ The world's deepest cave was only discovered in 2001.
✳ **Australia is 35 times the size of Great Britain.**
✳ The world's 29 monarchies rule over almost nine per cent of the world's population.
✳ **Earth is slowing down – in a few million years there won't be a leap year.**
✳ **David James** currently holds the record for top-flight clean sheets with 142.
✳ **The first known copyright was granted in 1486.**
✳ The human head contains 22 bones.
✳ **During a total solar eclipse the temperature can drop by six degrees Celsius.**
✳ The first written account of the Loch Ness Monster was made in 565AD.
✳ **Jack Black is the child of two rocket scientists.**
✳ We'll next see Halley's Comet in 2061.
✳ **Tiger cubs are only 40 per cent of the weight of a newborn human.**

* David Trezeguet's **96mph belter against Man United in 1998 is the most powerful shot ever recorded.**
* The break up of the Soviet Union has created 28 new nations. **Kuwait has the lowest death rate in the world.**
* Amazon.com stores almost three million books.

✳ **There are 188 skyscrapers in Hong Kong – the most in any city**

I'm looking for Hong Kong Phooey?

One in 10 of the world's population lives on an island.
* The Nintendo Wii weighs just 2lbs – the same as a bag of sugar.
✳ **Mammals are the only animals with flaps around the ears.**
✳ The Statue of Liberty is the largest hammered copper statue in the world.
✳ **The tallest nation in the world is the Watusis of Burundi.**
* Over 90 per cent of all fish caught are caught in the northern hemisphere.

✳ **Kenny Sansom was the last person with a moustache to score for England (against Finland in 1984)**

* **A grand piano can be played faster than an upright (spinet) piano.**
* A DVD can store 13 times more data than a CD.
✳ **The doors that cover US nuclear silos weigh 748 tons and open in 19 seconds.**
✳ France has won the most Olympic cycling gold medals.
✳ **One hundred years ago London was the largest city in the world.**

✳ **Kazakhstan** is home to the world's tallest chimney (420m).
✳ Just under half of Russia is covered in forest.
✳ **Japan's Shinkansen bullet trains reach speeds up to 186mph.**
✳ A VW Touareg can tow a Boeing 757.
✳ **In 1532, Henry VIII constructed the world's first indoor bowling lanes.**

On average, shark attacks happen in Australian seas 15 times a year

"Hi, I'm here for the auditions for the new *Jaws* film"

Aah, the sweet taste of belly fluff

DEAR NUTS,
While on a jaunt to Japan I came across this charmingly-named orange fizzy drink. What on earth is wrong with the Japanese? What kind of a name is this for a soft drink?

James Brodie, Wolverhampton

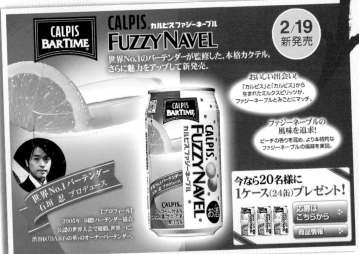

INADVERTENT RUDENESS

Pooh always had to do the donkey work

DEAR NUTS,
While out shopping, I noticed something rather strange on a Pooh Bear nightie in BHS. It seems as though Pooh and his friends have been enjoying some behind the scenes fun and games. What on earth would Christopher Robin say?

Jan Ryan, Great Barr

Eeyore does not look too happy about his part in proceedings, does he?

Ee by Gum

DEAR NUTS,
I came across this when I was eating a bag of Wine Gums. It made me giggle!

Phil Savage, Hertfordshire

The big questions are: did you pop it into your mouth for a chew? And if so, did you swallow?

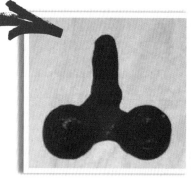

WARNING: LAWSUIT IMMINENT

DEAR NUTS,
I'm a big fan of the Hard Rock Café and I thought I'd found a new branch until I did a double take of this bar sign in Hua Hin, Thailand. They weren't serving the usual burgers and beers inside, I hasten to add.

Peter Crompton, Stevenage

At a guess, we'd imagine that ping pong balls came into play at some point…?

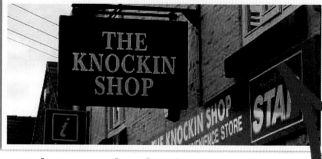

It does exactly what it says on the sign

DEAR NUTS,
I was driving through Wales recently, admiring the countryside when I spotted this shop – shame I had the girlfriend in the car with me!

Sam Toy, Essex

We've seen these before, but we've never seen one that had a post office in it too…

THE BEST OF SPAMBANK

CAT ON A HOT CHICK'S BOOB!

"Mmmmf... Can't... Move..."

SHOCKING SIGN

DANGER

HIGH VOLTAGE

IF YOU CAN CONVINCE THAT DRUNK GUY OVER THERE TO PEE ON THIS FENCE, YOU ARE IN FOR SOME SERIOUS LAUGHS

Don't try this at home. Or anywhere else

A ROMANTIC STROLL

My, how he's grown!

REAR VIEW

***Literally* a face like a dog's bum!**

PAYIN' IN THE BACKSIDE

ΤΗΛΕΔΙΟΔΙΟ E-PASS 2.7

ΚΑΡΤΑ ΔΙΟΔΙΩΝ SMART PASS

ΑΛΛΟΙ ΤΡΟΠΟΙ ΠΛΗΡΩΜΗΣ OTHER MEANS OF PAYMENT

Why you should *ALWAYS* have change in Greece...

For more hilarious pictures, go to...

NUTS.CO.UK/WEB

Nuts CLUB STRIP CHALLENGE

LOUISE
22 from Porthcawl

Hi, Louise. What type of men do you go for? Someone who's got a good personality and can make me laugh.

What's the best thing to do with your boobs? Touch them. Bite my nipples. Don't grope them, it's not nice.

What's the best way to give you an orgasm? Going downstairs. It feels so good.

Where's the strangest place you've done the deed? In some stables with some horses. Not actually with some horses, but on the farm where I keep them. It felt so naughty doing it in the hay.

Ever kissed a girl? Yes, when I was really drunk I snogged my friend. It was different, but I prefer boys.

What's the most embarrasing thing that's happened to you on a night out? I flashed my bum. I bent over too far and my dress came riding up!

Will you pull tonight? I'm looking good so I hope so.

What chance do boys like us have with a girl like you? Loads as long as you make me laugh

Thanks to Aqua, Cardiff

MIA

21 from Manchester

Hi, Mia. Have your boobs ever fallen out in a nightclub before?
I've only flashed my friends. Girls don't mind flashing in front of other girls.

What's the best way to chat you up?
Originality and humour. Tell me a funny joke. And don't try any cheesy chat-up lines.

Which do you prefer, snogging blokes or girls?
Girls are better. Women know what women want. I've kissed my friend, just for a laugh, nothing too serious. But she was a really good kisser.

What's your sexual fantasy?
A man in a fireman's outfit dancing for me!

Ever had sex in the toilets?
No. But I've had sex on a dining room table.

Was it in the middle of Sunday lunch?
No. It was in the middle of the day but nobody caught us and I didn't get any splinters!

Thanks to babesandboys. com at Café de Paris

For more gorgeous girls, go to...

NUTS.CO.UK/GIRLS

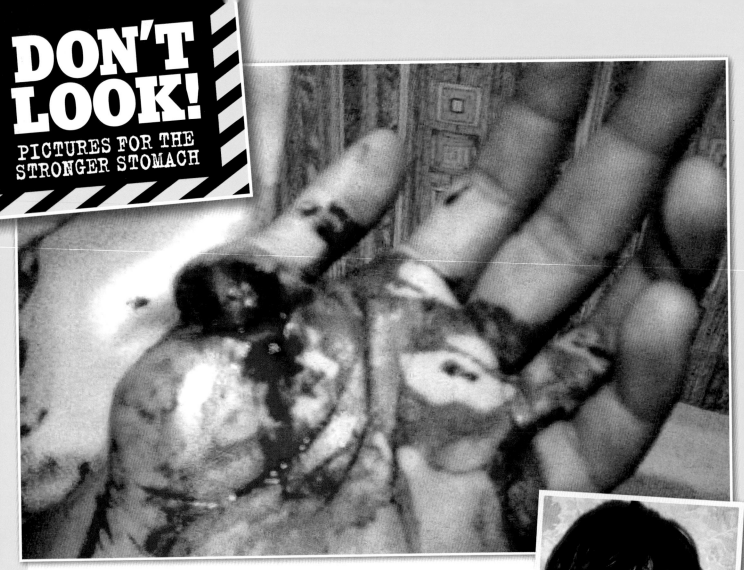

Reader's thumb nearly severed!

Nuts reader's thumb ripped off in drunken tiff

Normally, the worst pain you can expect from a heavy night out is a throbbing headache and a dodgy gut after that 3am kebab. Unfortunately for Resh Mohangee, 23, his drinking session left him in unbearable pain when he fell out with his brother.

"I was at home with my mates and my brother, Nash, but after a few too many beers, as usual, he started winding me up," Resh recalls. "He kept slamming the door in my face, so I stuck my hand in the way to stop him, but he slammed the door right on it. The impact was so hard it shattered the glass and nearly sliced my thumb clean off!"

With blood gushing everywhere, brother Nash called an ambulance. When they arrived at A&E, the doctors were so shocked by Resh's injuries that they immediately set to work repairing the damage.

"The doc said I was lucky to be alive, as I was close to severing a main artery. A team of surgeons took five hours to reattach the thumb and I had to be kept in for a further five days to recover."

Two months on, Resh has been left with major scarring, has little movement in his thumb and needs weekly physio. But he says it's not all bad: "I've been off work for six weeks and my brother's had to look after me. Also, he's giving slamming doors on people a miss from now on!"

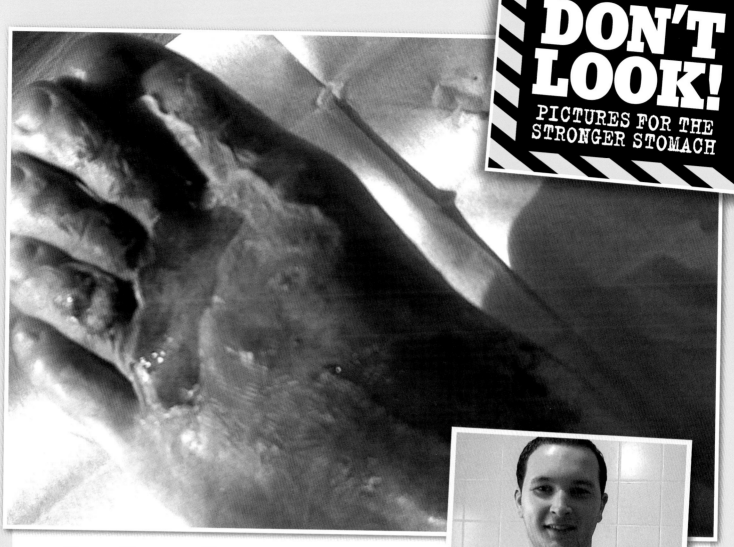

Bloke burns foot with boiling water

Scalding kettle goes berserk and douses reader's plates of meat

Don't you just love it when us blokes try to take a short cut to make things easy, only to have it all go horribly wrong and end in disaster.

Sadly, this is what happened to *Nuts* reader Mark Dennis when, while getting himself ready for a night out, he took a kettle full of boiling water into the bathroom after his hot water ran out.

"I poured half the water from the kettle into the bathroom sink, popped it on the loo and started shaving. Then the b*stard kettle slid off the toilet and doused my bare feet with scalding water.

"I was screaming, rushing to fill the bath with cold water and trying to phone my sister all at the same time. Eventually, I submerged my feet, but it was still so painful, I couldn't even look at them."

Luckily for Mark, 21, his sister was soon on the scene, closely followed by an ambulance.

"I was in so much pain, I couldn't walk, even after they'd given me morphine.

Four hours later, they wrapped my feet in cling film and wet cloths, and sent me home with some powerful painkillers."

A week on, Mark was still struggling to walk, and couldn't return to his job as a fishmonger – but it's not all bad: "I'll be off work for a while," he says, "so I can reacquaint myself with daytime TV." Good man.

19

Supercars

SSC Ultimate
Aero Turbo

The Aero is actually hand-made in the USA. Supercar-builder SSC made this Aero so they could attempt to beat the top-speed record for a road car – held by the Bugatti Veyron at a chin-trembling 253mph!

The "standard" Aero produces 787bhp and the "Ultimate" Aero puts out 1,046bhp, but the model shown here – used in the top-speed attempt – is the Ultimate Aero Turbo with 1,183bhp – That's nearly 400bhp more than a Formula One car!

Despite all this power, the SSC Ultimate Aero Turbo managed to reach "only" 230mph, a mere 23mph short of the Bugatti's top-speed record.
0–60mph in a mind-blowing 2.78 seconds!

The Ultimate Aero Turbo has a calculated top speed of 273mph – and the nutters at SSC are desperate to prove it…

"It doesn't take much to get me going!"

Michelle Marsh and her new photo shoot

Thank goodness for Michelle Marsh. She's so down to earth and approachable that all the girls want to meet her. After a few fireworks in the bedroom? Then you'd better ask Michelle.

So, Michelle, Do you ever wish you had smaller boobs? God yes, because then I wouldn't always have to wear a bra. If I don't wear a bra now they jiggle about too much and people stare.

Is there any other famous person's boobs you'd like? Carmen Electra's, even though they're fake, they're amazing. I love her boobs! Pinder's are great, too. Trust me, I've seen her nipples and they're the best boobs.

When was the last time that you knocked something over with your boobs? I hit people in the face with them by accident all the time I tried to weigh them in a supermarket once but got told off because it was on those scales where you weigh your fruit and veg..

What's the best thing about yours? You can get what you want with them. If someone says no to me I just say "pleeeease" and squeeze them together until they're irresistible. No one can say no after that…

Who are the hottest dressers? Definitely the Scouse girls! I ended up snogging a girl from Liverpool and her boyfriend fell out with her so if she's reading this, I'm so sorry!

Eh? What happened? We were on stage in this club playing games with strawberries and the girls were being really boring, so I kicked one off to take her place but ended up snogging this other girl as well!

"I snogged a girl from Liverpool – her bloke fell out with her!"

Have you done that before? What? Snogged a bird? Yes, quite a few times. I enjoy doing it.

What's the rudest thing you've ever seen in a club? I've had two girls wrestling in a paddling pool covered in baby oil, and two guys and two girls playing strip musical chairs. I've even had couples doing naked pole dancing.

What's the way to get you in the mood? I've been on a shoot and I'm all dolled up, I definitely feel a lot hornier when I get home than if I've been cleaning all day! But then I've got a very high sex drive anyway, so it doesn't take much to get me going.

If a bloke's meeting a girl for a first date, what should he wear to impress her? Baggy jeans and a nice T-shirt. No leather pants and definitely no tight vests, even if you have muscly arms.

Any tips if you want to try something new in the bedroom? Wet your finger when you're going down on your girlfriend and then lightly tickle that area between her front bum and back bum. It'll drive her absolutely bonkers!

Blimey! Have you ever got it on in a steam room then? Not as yet. The nearest I've got is on a booze cruise under a towel on the top deck. It was the middle of the day and there were loads of people around, which made it pretty daring.

Do you think you need any sex tips? I don't think I'm a pro but whoever I'm with always has a good relationship! Sex is important in every relationship and if you say otherwise then you're just in denial. I love dressing up and doing a striptease. You've got to have no inhibitions when it comes to being with your fella. Then it will be fantastic.

What do you prefer: modelling or singing? The modelling helped get me a record contract, so no matter what, I'll still be getting my boobs out for *Nuts!*

Nuts JOKES

Stay frosty!

A Best bottle opener

After striking gold in Alaska, a lonely miner walks down from the mountains and into a saloon in the nearest town. "I'm lookin' for the meanest, toughest, roughest hooker you got," he says to the barman.

"We got her," he replies. "She's upstairs in the second room on the right."

The miner hands the pint-puller a gold nugget to pay for the lady of the night and two beers. He grabs the bottles, stomps up the stairs, kicks open the door and yells, "I'm looking for the meanest, roughest, toughest hooker in town."

The woman inside the room looks at the miner and says, "You found her!"

Then she strips naked, bends over and grabs her ankles.

"How do you know I want that position first?" asks the miner.

"I don't," replies the hooker, "I just thought you might like to open those beers first."

Nathan Sutton, Nuneaton

Lying on a Sunday

A minister is winding up his sermon one Sunday in church.

"Next Sunday I'm going to preach on the subject of liars. And in this connection, as a preparation for my discourse, I would like you all to read the seventeenth chapter of Mark," he says.

On the following Sunday, the vicar walks to the front of the church and says, "Now, then, all of you who have done as I requested and read the seventeenth chapter of Mark, please raise your hands."

Nearly every hand in the congregation shoots up.

The vicar looks surprised and says, "You are the people I want to talk to about lying. There is no seventeenth chapter of Mark."

Frank Butters, Devon

The UFO cleared the M25 of all traffic

Q: What do you call a fat alien? A: An extra-cholesterol

Colin Wilson, via email

That sucks

A woman has been in a coma for several weeks, but one day nurses notice a slight response while washing her private parts. They rush to her husband and explain the surprise, suggesting a little oral sex might bring her round to which he readily agrees. A few minutes later her monitor flat lines, showing no pulse or heart rate. The nurses rush into the room crying "What happened!?"

"I'm not sure," the husband replies, "she may have choked".
Stu Baker, Hull.

Breakfast for two

Two Scottish businessmen walk into a cafe and order two cups of tea. Then they produce a plate each from their briefcases that contain a full English breakfast on each and begin to eat. The owner is amazed at their nerve and marches over. "You can't eat your own breakfasts in here!" he shouts.

The Scotsmen look at each other, shrug their shoulders and exchange plates.
Ben Meades, via email

Wot no beanz?

Portrait of a very smelly person's cupboard

Just chilling

Two men waiting at the Pearly Gates strike up a conversation.

"How'd you die?" the first man asks the second.

"I froze to death," says the second.

"That's awful," says the first man. "How does it feel to freeze to death?"

"It's very uncomfortable at first," says the second man. "You get the shakes, and you get pains in all your fingers and toes. But eventually, it's a very calm way to go. You get numb and you kind of drift off, as if you're sleeping. How about you, how did you die?"

"I had a heart attack," says the first man. "You see, I knew my wife was cheating on me, so one day I showed up at home unexpectedly. I ran up to the bedroom, and found her alone, knitting. I ran down to the basement, but no one was hiding there, either. I ran up to the second floor, but no one was hiding there either. I ran as fast as I could to the attic, and just as I got there, I had a massive heart attack and died."

The second man shakes his head. "That's so ironic," he says.

"What do you mean?" asks the first man.

"If you had only stopped to look in the freezer, we'd both still be alive, he replies."

A backward blonde

A blonde walks into a pharmacy and asks the pharmacist for some rectal deodorant. The pharmacist, a little confused, explains to the blonde that they don't sell rectal deodorant, and never have. Unfazed, the blonde assures the pharmacist that she has been buying the stuff from the store on a regular basis and would like some more.

"I always buy it here," says the blonde.

"Do you have the container that it came in?" asks the pharmacist.

"Yes, I've got my old one here," says the blonde. She hands it to the pharmacist. "This is just a normal stick of underarm deodorant," he says to her.

Annoyed, the blonde snatches the container back and reads out loud from the container: "To apply, push bottom up."
Danny West, Sheffield

LADIES CONFESS

TO OUR SECRETARY

"He pulled my skirt up around my waist"

My friends were chatting in a café when four sexy men wandered in. Immediately, I locked eyes with one of them. It was clear we were attracted to each other. We started chatting and arranged to meet up later. I went home, showered and smothered myself in body lotion. I felt very horny. We met in a park nearby and he arrived looking sexier than I remembered, his muscles strained against his tight shirt. I couldn't help myself, so I kissed him passionately, my tongue darting into his mouth. His member was rock hard and rubbing against me. He pulled my skirt up around my waist and started sliding his fingers in and out of me. I was

dripping wet and climaxed almost immediately – I didn't even have time to undo his zip!
Rosie, Wallsend

"He took me over the car"

After a night out, my partner and I stopped for a bit of outdoor passion. It was late and no one was around, so we parked in an industrial estate. We got out of the car and started to kiss. He threw me over the car's bonnet, flung my skirt up and lifted my knickers. We enjoyed some role-play where I played the naughty girlfriend, while he spanked me. He got on top of me and placed himself inside me. We both came in no time. Half-naked, we stood and cuddled. It was exciting – until I looked up and saw the CCTV camera pointing right at

us. I can't help wondering if there's a security guard out there who enjoyed himself almost as much as we did!
Maureen, Scotland

"Biting my lip, I tried not to scream"

Last weekend, my boyfriend had to work, so I decided to pay him a "special visit" dressed in high-heeled black boots and a little skirt without any underwear. I walked into his office and he was all over me immediately, kissing the back of my neck with his hands roaming everywhere. Turning around, I pulled down his trousers and saw that he was already really hard. He bent me over the desk and began to stroke my clitoris, and I could feel myself becoming really wet. I grabbed hold of the desk and bit my lip as he took me. It was all I could do not to cry out with pleasure. Afterwards, he was full of satisfied smiles, so I'm sure I'll be making many more work visits!
Amy, Bath

> **"He bent me over the desk"**

"We did it up against a wall"

I went round to my fella Tom's house but he was still stuck at

work. I decided to wait and his flatmate got me a glass of wine. We got on well and I'd always thought he was pretty fit. After a few hours, Tom called and said he was staying at his mate's as no trains were running. I got up to leave, but his flatmate squeezed my hand. I stood up and we started kissing. I could feel him rubbing against me and it was such a turn-on. He pulled off my clothes and gave me the best head I'd ever had. I pulled off his trousers and put my mouth around his member and we were soon doing it up against a wall. I split up with Tom a few weeks later and never saw his flatmate again, but what a memory!
Anna, Plymouth

"I had no knickers on"

My boyfriend's 21st birthday was coming up and I decided to give him a special treat. He was staying at my house, so I got up extra early to give him something to remember. I gave my private area a shave, turning myself on as I went along and spent ages moisturising myself and paying a lot of attention to my breasts. Then, I got dressed up in my sexiest schoolgirl outfit and prepared a breakfast he wouldn't forget. Instead of toast and a cup of tea, I

had a tray of champagne, strawberries and cream and a selection of lubes and naughty toys to play with. I woke him up with me sitting over his face with no knickers on, dripping wet. Let's just say, we didn't leave the bedroom all day and he won't ever forget that birthday.
Rosie, Birmingham

"I climaxed in seconds"

I'd just returned from a holiday without my boyfriend so when we saw each other again, we were both really horny. We decided to go swimming at a local hotel. We messed about in the pool kissing and touching each other, which got us really turned on. We then sneaked back into the blokes' changing rooms and before I knew it, he slipped his hands down my bikini bottoms where I was already very wet. Gasping, we checked the door and I climbed on top of him. The excitement of where we were and the fact we could have been caught at any minute meant we both climaxed in seconds. It was definitely the sexiest changing room I've ever been in!
Victoria, Blackpool

"I could feel myself getting very wet"

I started a job at the same place my partner works and we ended up doing a lot more than just work. One lunchtime, we were left alone in the warehouse. We were in a flirtatious mood, so we moved to the staff area. I was feeling very horny and judging by the bulge in his pants, so was he. We started kissing and one thing led to another. I undid his

trousers, pulled out his enormous manhood and started sucking it hard. He pulled down my trousers, bent me over the table and stroked my hot spot. I could feel myself getting very wet. He took me hard from behind and I bit my lip trying not to cry out with pleasure. We both came soon afterwards. I had a satisfied smile on my face all day. I look forward to doing it again!
Angela, Worcester

"He lifted my skirt and began licking"

Late one afternoon, my boss and I were working in the office when a phone engineer came in to check a dodgy phone line. He was gorgeous! I caught his eye as he walked in, and instantly felt horny. The phone socket was under my desk and as he crawled under, I sat back in my chair and spread my legs, to see what he'd do. Quietly, he lifted my skirt, pulled my thong to one side and started to lick me. I came so hard but had to keep quiet so that my boss didn't know what was going on. A few minutes later, my boss left for the day, after instructing me to look after the engineer. So, I did just that! I unzipped his trousers and leaned forward over the desk. He slid into me, hot and hard, and I came instantly. It was definitely the best day I've ever had at work!
Jacqui, Milton Keynes

"He put his hand inside my skirt"

Last summer, my boyfriend and I were driving back from our holiday with his family. To take my mind off the heat, I decided to read a book, not realising how

> **"I unzipped his trousers and leaned forward over the desk"**

steamy it was. I began to get very aroused and got myself even hotter. My boyfriend looked over to see why I was getting so restless and I saw his face light up as his eyes skimmed the pages in front of me. He then slyly put his hand inside my skirt and stroked me with his fingers. I was literally biting my tongue to stop myself from screaming out with pleasure. The thrill of knowing we could be caught at any minute lead me to an intense orgasm. Eventually, I had to stop him before his family caught on to our saucy back-seat antics. Now, whenever I get in the car with his family I can't help but smile.
Julia, Southampton

"We all began touching each other"

My boyfriend and I went away for the weekend with my best friend and her boyfriend. While we were in the hotel steam room, I sat in between my boyfriend's legs and started playing with his manhood, feeling him getting more and more aroused. I let out a moan as he started playing with my nipples. Suddenly, the door opened and my best friend and her boyfriend were standing there watching. I could see a bulge forming in his shorts and before I knew it, they were beside us touching each other. My boyfriend pulled aside my bikini bottoms and bent me over and my best friend's boyfriend decided he wanted some, too. I was sucking him off as my best friend played with herself. There must have been about six orgasms between all of us before we all collapsed on the bench in a sweaty mess.
Nicki, London

We all like to see what the sexiest Real Girls in the UK get up to in their bedrooms, don't we? Well here's a selection of the best of the best...

30

BEDROOM BABES

CRYSTAL

25, from Warrington, promotions

"I like a man with a sense of humour and good manners. A witty gentleman. I don't like macho types."

BEDROOM BABES

SOFFINA

19, from Birmingham, student

"Because of my Scandinavian roots, the sauna's one of my favourite places. The thought of sexy fun in there gets me hot and bothered."

BEDROOM
BABES
TIA
21, from Derby, hairdresser

"If I'm feeling adventurous in the bedroom, I'll wear a pair of fishnet stockings, a basque and some suspenders. That really gets me in the mood!"

BEDROOM BABES
LOUISE
22, from Doncaster, sales manager

"You need to take it easy when you're in bed with me. Lots of kissing and tickling is good. And spend some time down there..."

BEDROOM BABES

DANIELLA

19, from Epsom, office manager

"I like dressing up as a nurse. It's a nice mix of tenderness, because it's a caring profession, and being really naughty."

BEDROOM BABES

KATIE

19, from Bury St Edmonds, beauty therapist

"I'm single at the moment and on the lookout for a guy. I like tall, pretty boys with a good personality. So, if you fit the bill, come over and say hello!"

BEDROOM BABES

NICOLA

20, from Manchester, student

"The best way to get me interested is to make me laugh. Looks come second to a great sense of humour."

Nuts WEIRD STUFF

Two-faced pig!

We love our freakish animals here at *Nuts*, and you'll find none freakier than this young chap! As you can see, it's a pig with more than the usual complement of heads. They do say that two is better than one, and the pig's Chinese owners certainly agree – what with it being Year Of The Pig in China, they're hailing it as some sort of miracle. All we can think is, "Mmm. More bacon!"

PINK *AND* PERKY

Croc loves man!

Here's a love story to charm the hardest heart. Gilberto and Pocho have been inseparable for 17 years, so close that huge crowds flock to watch them frolic. The twist? Gilberto's a Costa Rican fisherman, and Pocho's a 15-foot crocodile. Gilberto found young Pocho with a bullet in his head, nursed him back to health, and now they're best friends. And Pocho hasn't eaten Gilberto. Yet.

BEST PALS!

World's biggest motorbike!

Just look at the size of this bad boy! Officially the tallest rideable motorcycle in the world, it's a 15ft-high, 25ft-long, six-and-a-half ton, £155,000 beast. In order to "ride" it, you have to climb into a cockpit below the handlebars. The owner, Gregory Dunham of Stockton, USA, built it for a dare. We assume he won.

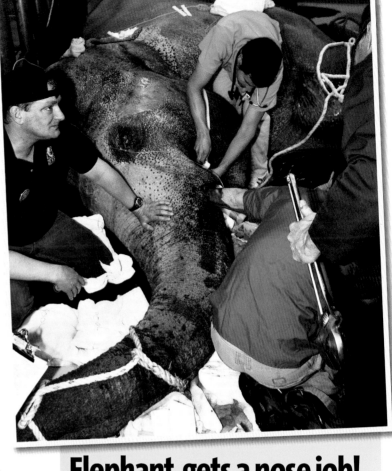

Elephant gets a nose job!

You may wonder why this man is almost up to his elbow in an elephant's face. Well, Tusko the elephant, from Oregon Zoo, USA, is receiving medical treatment to remove an infected tusk. We're guessing that he'll have to change his name now.

MORE WEIRD STUFF

For more true stories, go to...

NUTS.CO.UK/WEB

FOOTBALL QUOTES

"It's a hell of a long journey home and we got three points – take it off us now if you can. You can't!"

Don't worry Ian Holloway, Plymouth's three points for their win at Colchester are safe.

"I'll take any goal, any time, any place, anywhere – you can call me the Martini striker."

West Ham forward Carlton Cole gives himself a truly ridiculous nickname.

"Look, I'm just here to buy a house shaped like a penis."

Peter Crouch on Rio Ferdinand's World Cup Windups on ITV1.

"Isn't it lovely to see a pair of strikers playing with each other."

David Pleat. Need we say more?

"I was in the kitchen making a sandwich. I was in so much shock afterwards, I couldn't tell you what kind of sandwich it was."

Charlton's Darren Bent on his freak finger-cutting injury.

"It's not far from London, so he can just get up off his lazy a*se and get down here and watch his son."

"Bradley Wright-Phillips sends a subtle message to his old man Ian.

"I love films. Yesterday I saw *Hostel*. Don't watch! I was in my bed with the sheets pulled up."

Maybe Bernardo Corradi should try watching Pride & Prejudice next time.

"People need to understand what kind of goldfish Wayne Rooney lives in."

Thank you, Graham Taylor.

"I don't read the papers, I don't gamble. I don't even know what day it is."

Steve McClaren, one of the front-runners for the England job.

"And here's Jose Mourinho talking to the Chelsea manager Garth Crooks."

Radio Five Live's DJ Spoony with shock news.

I know boss – get Becks back!

Must... clean... balls

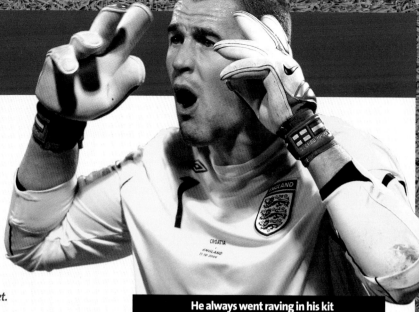
He always went raving in his kit

worried about a game that lets its players do that in public."

Ian Holloway on cricket.

"As I see it, the bowler bowls the ball. Then he gets it back and rubs it on his groin. I've always been a bit

"My Sky box is knackered and they've told me they can't fix it until mid-

December. If they can't be bothered to come out, I'm not going to do any interviews."

David James will be writing to Watchdog next.

"It's been a long, hard thing for me."

Harry Kewell on his groin problems.

"It's seven years today, my anniversary, and it was my birthday yesterday – it's been a great weekend for me. I better be careful with the missus otherwise I'll probably put her in the club."

Neil Warnock on seven years at Bramall Lane.

"It's like a big yellow banana running at you!"

Mark Lawrenson gets fruity about Paul Robinson.

"I used to love that cartoon when I was a kid that had a fella called Dick Dastardly. He had a wonderful dog called Mutley and a little fella who was his ideas person who used to go, "We're going to ripwhoopboom that pigeon." I've got one or two who went like that.

Criticising players, Ian Holloway style.

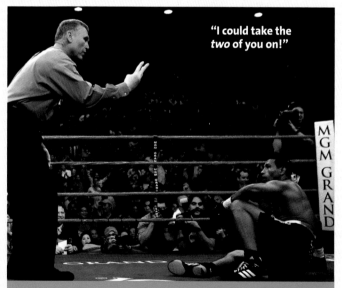
"I could take the *two* of you on!"

"I am going to knock him out, but I want to stop his heart or detatch a retina – one of the two."

Friendly pre-fight trash talk from Ricardo Mayorga – who then took a fearful beating from Oscar De La Hoya.

43

Nuts CLUB STRIP CHALLENGE

DION
23, from Cwmbran

Hi Dion, Have you boobs ever fallen out in a nightclub?
"I got a bit rude with my boyfriend once but no one noticed. It wasn't full-on but it was near enough.

Ever thrown up over someone you fancy? SI've thrown up after kissing someone I fancied. I snogged him and then I was like, "hold on a second, bleeeugh!" and was sick everywhere. That was fun!

Worst chat-up line? Being from Wales, you hear so many. They're all bad at chatting up in Wales.

Which is best: snogging blokes or snogging girls? Girls! Actually, I've kissed one tonight! She was really hot and a great kisser.

What snogging tips can us boys pick up from you girls? Take it slower. Boys like to steam right in. It should be more about the build-up.

Rudest sexual fantasy? A big orgy with a load of sexy females!

What will your friends think when they see you in _Nuts_?
They'll love it! They'll be really proud of me.

Thanks to babesandboys.com at Café de Pariain Bristol

LAUREN
18 from Winchester

Hi Lauren. Have your boobs fallen out in a nightclub before? No. I only flash my boobs on a beach. I don't like to get tan lines.

You told us you are recently single. What sort of bloke are you looking for? Someone who's romantic and generous. I'm not a gold-digger – just buy me dinner occasionally!

Best way to chat you up? Buy me a drink and chat to me rather than looking at my boobs. And don't use cheesy chat-up lines.

Which is best: snogging blokes or snogging girls? Girls kiss slowly and passionately. I've kissed a lot of my girlfriends. Most boys kiss too fast. They eat your face off.

Weirdest place you've had sex? In my ex's Metro, probably. Ha ha!

Sexual fantasy? Top of the Eiffel Tower, in the revolving restaurant. I'd like the risk!

What will your friends say when they see you in *Nuts*? They'll probably laugh!

Thanks to babesandboys. com at Café de Paris

45

US sport's biggest earners

1 DAVID BECKHAM (MLS/SOCCER) – $50 MILLION A YEAR

Goldenballs decision to play for LA Galaxy has catapulted him straight to the top of the big earners' club throughout all the US Leagues. His deal works out at £50 a minute – that means 90 minutes at The Home Depot Stadium will net him £4,500.

2 MICHAEL VICK (NFL/AMERICAN FOOTBALL) – $23.1 MILLION A YEAR

Even though he didn't make the Super Bowl this year the Atlanta Falcons' quarterback still picks up the biggest pay cheque in Gridiron.

3 ALEX RODRIGUEZ (MLB/BASEBALL) – $21.7 MILLION A YEAR

The New York Yankees' fabled hitter, nicknamed A-Rod, is one of the team's many baseball superstars, although his earning power isn't what it used to be – he now has to exist on under £13 million a year.

4 KEVIN GARNETT (NBA/BASKETBALL) – $21 MILLION/YEAR

The towering 6ft 11 power forward who plays for the Minnesota Timberwolves is basketball's highest paid star. 'The Big Ticket' was the first NBA player to be snapped up while still in High School.

5 DEREK JETER (MLB/BASEBALL) – $20.6 MILLION A YEAR

The captain of the New York Yankees and the closest thing to Beckham in baseball. All that cash works wonders with the women too. Jeter's gone through a string of babes from Mariah Carey, a Miss Universe, an MTV presenter and is currently dating actress Jessica Biel.

Lord and Lady Cheese

He took rounders very seriously

6 JASON GIAMBI (MLB/BASEBALL) – $20.4 MILLION A YEAR

Another Yankee. No surprise that the New York team have got the same reputation as Chelsea for trying to buy glory. All-rounder Giambi could have chosen basketball or American football as a career but decided on baseball.

7 SHAQUILLE O'NEAL (NBA/BASKETBALL) – $20 MILLION A YEAR

Shaq is the 7ft 1 Miami Heat legend who has been playing at the highest level of the game since he burst on to the scene in 1992 with the Orlando Magic.

=8 MATT HASSELBECK (NFL/AMERICAN FOOTBALL) – $19 MILLION A YEAR

The Seattle Seahawks' quarterback and his team were Super Bowl losers last year. This year he justified his salary by leading them as far as the quarterfinals.

=8 MIKE MUSSINA (MLB/BASEBALL) – $19 MILLION A YEAR

Another Yankees starter and one of the best pitchers in baseball history, Mussina, nicknamed The Moose, is a six-time Gold Glove Award winner. That means he's quite good.

10 ORLANDO PACE (NFL/AMERICAN FOOTBALL) – $18 MILLION A YEAR

The 6ft 7, 325lb offensive tackle for the St Louis Rams is a one-time Super Bowl winner and inventor of the "Pancake block" where he hits an opponent so hard they collapse as a flat as one.

SOURCE: MLS/NFL/MLB/NBA

Big money 'best picture' Oscar winners

Movies that swept the board at the box office and awards

1 TITANIC – £952,500,000 WORLD BOX OFFICE

Apart from the prestigious Best Picture award this water-bound weepy, beloved by girlfriends everywhere, snaffled another ten Academy Awards and enough dosh to earn the title: "Highest grossing film of all time."

2 LORD OF THE RINGS: THE RETURN OF THE KING – £559,450,000 WORLD BOX OFFICE

The final installment in Peter Jackson's trilogy won all the categories it was nominated for equalling Ben-Hur and Titanic for the most Oscars ever won by a single film.

3 FORREST GUMP – £338,700,000 WORLD BOX OFFICE

Tom Hanks played the fool and walked away with his second Oscar for Best Actor. The film got 13 nominations at the 1994 Awards, bagging six statues.

4 GLADIATOR – £228,800,000 WORLD BOX OFFICE

Ridley Scott's historical action epic more than made up for its budget of £52 million and the character of Maximus Decimus Meridius also bagged Russell Crowe an Oscar.

5 DANCES WITH WOLVES – £212,100,000 WORLD BOX OFFICE

The highest-grossing Western of all time did the business at the box office and at the 1990 Oscars, where it won seven awards, including Best Picture and Best Director for Kevin Costner.

6 RAIN MAN – £208,000,000 WORLD BOX OFFICE

Hoffman and Cruise dubbed the film Two Schmucks and Car because they didn't think it would be successful. It went on to win five awards, including an acting award for Hoffman.

7 GONE WITH THE WIND – £201,100,000 WORLD BOX OFFICE

This 1939 epic still competes with today's modern blockbusters and, when inflation is taken into account, it's the biggest money making film in history. It held the record for ten Oscars, before *Titanic's* glory.

8 AMERICAN BEAUTY – £176,150,000 WORLD BOX OFFICE

The Kevin Spacey drama was a huge artistic and commercial success and director Sam Mendes went on to direct *The Road to Perdition* and *Jarhead*.

9 SCHINDLER'S LIST – £162,150,000 WORLD BOX OFFICE

Steven Spielberg's biopic of Oskar Schindler was an Oscar-cert almost before any one had even seen it. It won seven Oscars including Spielberg's first for directing.

10 A BEAUTIFUL MIND – £157,260,000 WORLD BOX OFFICE

A year after *Gladiator* Russell Crowe got another nomination but missed out to Denzel Washington in *Training Day*. The film was still awarded four Oscars, including Best Picture.

Wayne Rooney's diet wasn't working out

Greenest cars in the UK

No Lamborghini Murcielago then?

1 Toyota Prius – 104 g of CO2/km
2 Citroen C2 – 108 g of CO2/km
3 Citroen C3 – 110 g of CO2/km
=3 Renault Clio – 110 g of CO2/km
5 Smart Fortwo – 113 g of CO2/km
=5 Peugeot 206 – 113 g of CO2/km
7 Ford Fiesta 1.4 – 114 g of CO2/km
=7 Daihatsu Charade – 114 g of CO2/km
9 Audi A2 – 116 g of CO2/km
=9 Honda Civic – 116 g of CO2/km

Bendiest roads in Britain

1 B3081, Cann Common to Tollard Royal – 352kNs of force
2 A686, Penrith to Melmerby – 276kNs of force
3 A537, Macclesfield to Buxton – 221kNs of force
4 A466, Monmouth to Staunton – 195kNs of force
5 A4061, Pricetown to Treorchy – 167kNs of force
6 A157, Louth to Mablethorpe – 152kNs of force
7 B2130, Godalming to Cranleigh – 151kNs of force
8 B6270, Keld to Reeth, 128 – kNs of force
9 A39, Bridgewater to Minehead – 118kNs of force
=9 B797, Mennock to Warnlockhead – 99kNs of force

SOURCES: BOXOFFICEMOJO.COM, MSN, CONTINENTAL TYRES

FOOTBALL'S FITTEST FANS

We get to the bottom of what makes female football fans so special

EMMA
21, from Tamworth
SUPPORTS: England

Come off you reds!… and black and whites, and blues and in fact, everything. We reckon the next six pages contain the fittest football fans ever seen. What do you think?

STACEY
20, from Stoke-on-Trent
SUPPORTS: Arsenal

MICHELLE
21, from Lewisham
SUPPORTS: Liverpool

CLARE
18, from Wembley
SUPPORTS: Arsenal

FOOTBALL'S FITTEST FANS

LAUREN
23, from Manchester
SUPPORTS: Man United

LAURA
22, from North Wales
SUPPORTS: Blackburn

HOLLY
20, from Liverpool
SUPPORTS: Everton

TANYA
21, from North Wales
SUPPORTS: Liverpool

51

FOOTBALL'S FITTEST FANS

SAMMI
20, from Canterbury
SUPPORTS: Chelsea

53

Mental Porsche!

The new RUF CTR3 is a radically modified supercar based on the Porsche 911!

The engine is positioned in the middle, not the rear like the 911 – and kicks out a staggering 700bhp at 7,000rpm!

That's what you get when you twin turbocharge a 3.8-litre flat six-cylinder engine!

The CTR3 is aerodynamically designed for high speed, and the sleek bodywork cuts through the air efficiently and delivers a top speed of 235mph!

The speedo goes up to 260mph!

The CTR3's top speed is 235mph and it does 0–60mph in just 3.2seconds!

The CTR3's bodywork is made from steel, aluminium and carbon-kevlar.

There's an integrated roll cage and side-impact protection beams should you make a monumental driving error…

The suspension uses racing car-style coilovers and the brake discs are a massive 380mm!

The wheels are equally huge, with 19-inch rims up front and giant 20-inch alloys at the rear.

The interior can be tailored to the customer's taste and there's a tasty aluminium gear shift lever for the sequential shift transmission.

How much for all this performance? That'll be around £300,000, sir…

MAN-LOVE

"I always loved going up the Arsenal, you know"

VIEIRA SLIPS INSIDE HIS MAN

Italy's celebrations go too far

ACTUAL DRY HUMPING

ACTUAL KISSING

Francesco Totti was always happy to see the kit man

Ecuador's training methods raised more than a few eyebrows

Preston get passionate.

"I CAN SEE RIGHT UP YOUR NOSE FROM HERE"

PACHUCO FC WEDDING?

"Blimey, you've piled on the pounds!"

Franck Ribery of Marseille gets a "special" group hug

ROO REALLY LOVES RON

"I know you didn't mean to get me sent off you big softie"

THEY LOVE TEAM BONDING

"Well maybe just the one"

"What are you doing?" "Making sure you don't get cramp, obviously." "Oh. Right"

F. TORRES 9

NO TONGUES

REAL GIRLS TALK

Louise 21, DONCASTER

Q: How would you use food with your guy?
"Well, I absolutely adore chocolate, so I'd love to spread it all over my man and take loads of time licking it all off his quivering body! I think I'd probably start at his belly button and work my way down from there. Mmm!"

Cheryl-Marie 24, YORKSHIRE

Q: Would you consider something new during a one-night stand? "Yeah, most one-night stands happen when you're out on the town, so people are drunk, feel sexy and are more adventurous. I'm not shy when it comes to sex and and one-night stands are a great way to experiment."

Charlotte 20, BILLERICAY

Q: Where do women most like to be kissed?
"Apart from the mouth, women like to be kissed on the tops of their legs. Once your partner starts kissing you there, you know they're going "downstairs". Kissing girls on their nipples is also a surefire way to turn us on."

Becky 20, LONDON

Q: Ever had a one-night stand with more than one person at a time? "I met this gorgeous guy on a girlie night out. He whispered in my ear, "Would you be interested in having a threesome?" I called over one of my girly mates, and all three of us went back to his hotel room. It was sexy, steamy and fun!"

58

SEX! Saucy babes share their steamy secrets!

Ellie 24, LONDON

Q: Do you think aphrodisiacs work? "What happens when you eat one? My boyfriend and I heard that pearl lollies are a good aphrodisiac, so we tried it for a laugh. I'm not sure if it was all that licking and sucking, but I couldn't wait to get him into bed that night!"

100% REAL

Emma 18, LANCASHIRE

Q: What wouldn't you do on a one-night stand? "I wouldn't want to hand over all I have to someone I don't even know. I don't get anything out of just sex. I prefer sex to be part of a relationship where you can relax and explore things that you are happy and comfortable doing together you can have much more fun."

Kelly 25, CAMBRIDGE

Q: How should men use their tongues? "Tongues are a major sex tool and if guys happen to be lacking in the "downstairs department" then good use of the tongue can really rescue the situation. Let's get this straight, though, a slobbery kiss is never good."

DID YOU KNOW?

● One-night stands allow you to act out your fantasies and try out things you may be too scared to do with someone you know.

● Sex for its own sake can be fun – providing you're playing safely (use condoms) and both know what you're getting into beforehand.

● If you want to make an impression, don't drink too much or you may get brewer's droop and have poor sex. On the plus side, you probably won't remember it in the morning.

● Be open about your intentions before you get up close and personal. She may think it's going to blossom into an amazing relationship while you just want a night of fun.

● If you meet a lady be polite and tell her friends where you are off to. They won't worry about her and they'll think you have nice manners. Plus, you may be in with a chance with one of them at a later stage.

● If you are going out on the pull, make sure your bedroom is smelling clean and looking tidy in case you get lucky.

● Have a plan ready for the morning in case you need to "be somewhere" or "have an appointment" to keep.

REAL GIRLS TALK SEX!

Cara 21, ABERDEEN

Q: Best kissing techniques? "I can tell instantly when my boyfriend is in the mood by the way he kisses me. My favourite is when he holds me quite roughly and the way he uses his tongue makes me go weak. I love it when I can feel stubble. That's a real turn-on."

Natalie 19, ST HELENS

Q: Is using food sexy, or just plain messy? "I think it's really sexy, because there are so many things you can try out – from whipped cream to warm honey. There are also loads of different textures to play around with against the skin. I love it and I don't care about a bit of mess!"

Emma-Lou 22, SOUTHAMPTON

Q: Would you be up for trying something new on a one-night stand? "Most definitely, I think it's an ideal time to try new things and let your inhibitions go. I don't do one-nighters, but me and my boyfriend try all sorts of exciting things and I love dressing up in naughty outfits."

Nicola 21, RUGBY

Q: What's the weirdest food you've used in sex?
"I once used a Snickers chocolate bar during sex, which I know sounds a bit weird! I was using it as a vibrator with a guy and it felt really sexy. I suppose it all got a bit messy but I got quite a lot of help licking it up, if you know what I mean!"

Danielle 19, SUNDERLAND

Q: Would you ever have a one-night stand?
I've never had a one-night stand and I really do not intend to do so. All the men I have slept with have been boyfriends, who at the time meant a lot to me.

100% REAL

Charlotte 23, PORTSMOUTH

Q: Do you like kissing during sex? "Kissing is really important, the soft sensual touching of tongues can work any girl into a frenzy when done right! The missionary position is the best to start with and I like a little kissing when I'm on top as that way it's me in charge."

FOODY SEX TIPS

● Why not let your lady hold a bottle of whipped cream and get her to place the cream wherever she wants you to lick her? It's a really good way to discover her erogenous zones and seeing how far she's willing to take things!

● If you need a quick and easy idea, then get some strawberries and champagne. Every girl loves bubbly and you can pour it over her and enjoy licking it off!

● Spare a thought for your girl when she's "downstairs". Spicy food and beer can make semen taste unpleasant, so drink a nice pineapple juice to make it sweet!

● If you're going to cover each other in chocolate and lick it off, don't buy cheap stuff — get a luxury Belgian bar.

● Aphrodisiacs are foods which are thought to make you really horny so stock up on oysters, asparagus and other supposedly horn-inducing grub like "pearl lollies" to set up a steamy evening. For more info on pearl lollies, see www.lazyboneuk.com or www.gourmetsleuth.com/aphrodis_foods.htm for a huge list of lots more aphrodisiacs!

● The erotic power of food has been celebrated for centuries. The famous 18th century womaniser, Casanova, was said to have shared oysters with his lovers to whet their sexual appetites, while Greek and Roman cultures enjoyed

EXCLUSIVE
BABE SHOTS!

These photographs have never been published before. Feast your eyes on them and don't say we never give you anything, you lucky people...

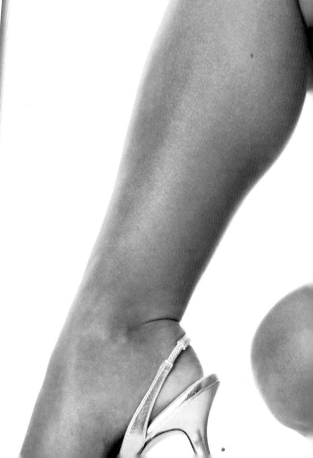

Naomi

Cara

Michelle and Cara

Sophie

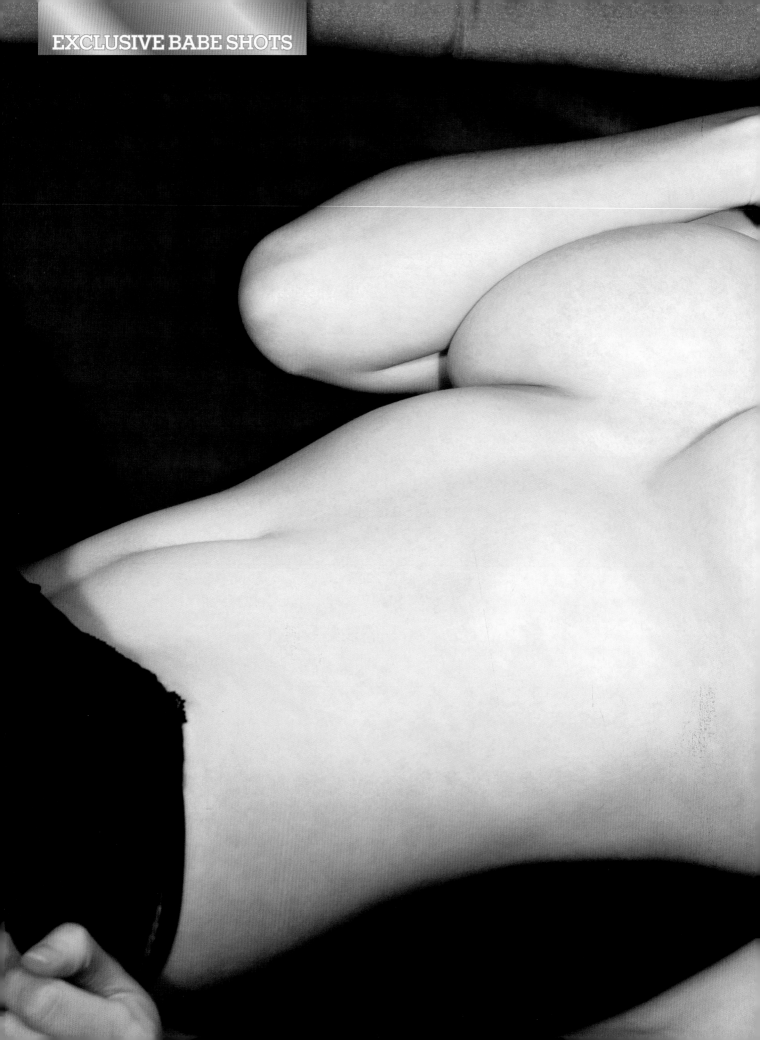

NutsJOKES

He's got it licked

Three guys are on a trip to Saudi Arabia. One day, they stumble into a harem tent with over 100 beautiful women inside. They start getting friendly with all the women, when suddenly the Sheik storms in.

"I am the master of all these women. No one else can touch them except me. You three

men must pay for what you have done today. You will be punished in a way corresponding to your profession."

The Sheik turns to the first man and asks him what he does for a living.

"I'm a policeman," says the first man.

"Then we will shoot your penis off!" says the Sheik.

He then turns to the second man and asks him what he did for a living.

"I'm a fireman," says the second man.

"Then we will burn your penis off!" says the Sheik.

Finally, he asks the last man, "And you, what do you do for a living?"

And the third man answers, "I'm a lollipop salesman!"

Off-colour

A sailor is driven off course by a storm, and smashes into a small island. The next morning, he awakes on the beach. The sand and sky are reddish. Walking around in a daze, the sailor sees red birds, red grass, red trees and red bananas. He is shocked to find that even his skin is red.

"Oh, no!" he exclaims. "I'm marooned!"

Teed off

A priest, a doctor, and a lawyer are waiting one morning on a particularly slow group of golfers.

"What's wrong with these guys?" fumes the lawyer. "We must have been waiting for 15 minutes!"

"I don't know," say the doctor, "but I've never seen such ineptitude!"

"Here comes the greenskeeper," says the priest. "Let's have a word with him.

"Say, George, what's with that group ahead of us? They're rather slow aren't they?"

"Oh, yes," says George, "That's the group of blind firemen. They lost their sight while saving our club last year. We let them play here anytime free of charge!"

Everyone is silent for a moment.

Then the priest says, "That's so sad, I think I'll say a prayer for them tonight."

"And I'm going to contact my ophthalmologist buddy and see if there is anything he can do for them," the doctor adds.

"Why can't the selfish bastards damn well play at night?" asks the lawyer.

Diamonds are a man's best friend

A doctor walks into a bank. Preparing to sign a cheque, he accidentally pulls a rectal thermometer out of his shirt pocket and tries to write with it. Realising his mistake, he looks at the thermometer with annoyance and says, "Well, that's just great. Some asshole's got my pen!"

To which the faithful servant replies, "Ugg ou gery muk."

Longest sentence in the English language? Will you marry me?

Q: What do you call a woman who knows where her husband is?
A: A widow.

Not just a pretty smell...

eau de toilette

Miller Harris
PERFUMER LONDON

figue amere

50 ml e 3.4 fl oz.

Classy girls

Two Aussie girls walk up to the perfume counter in a superstore and pick up a sample bottle.

Shazza sprays it on her wrist and smells it: "That's quite nice, don't you think Cheryl?"

"Yeah, what's it called?" says Cheryl to the assistant.

"Viens a moi," comes the reply.

"Viens a moi, what does that mean?" quips Shazza.

"Viens a moi, ladies, is French for 'come to me'," says the assistant haughtily.

Shazza takes another sniff and offers her arm to Cheryl saying, "That doesn't smell like come to me, does that smell like come to you, Cheryl?"

Servant takes large cut

A brave knight has to go off to fight in the Crusades and leaves his sexy wife at home. As she can't be left alone he fits her with a very lethal chastity belt made out of razor blades. On his victorious return, he lines up all his male staff, and makes them drop their trousers. He is greeted by a whole line of shredded todgers, apart from one. He goes up to the man and says, "I trusted you and unlike all the others, you have not betrayed my trust. In return I shall give you half my land."

To which the faithful servant replies, "Ugg ou gery muk."

Q: There are two cowboys in the kitchen. Which is the real one?
A: The one on the range.

Par for the course

A Catholic, Protestant and Mormon are sitting on a flight, talking about their families. The Catholic says, "I have ten kids at home and if I had another one I'd have a football team!"

"Well," says the Protestant, "I have 15 kids at home and if I had another one I'd have an American Football team."

"Well," said the Mormon, "I have 17 wives at home."

He paused, sipping at his drink. "If I had another one I'd have a golf course."

Nuts
WEIRD STUFF

Man Pulls Car With Ears!

Well, if you're not going to wear it, you can always do this: This Chinese gentleman's unique talent is attaching clips to his ears, attaching cords to the clips, attaching the cords to a car and then riding off on his motorbike, pulling the car along with his ears. It's a talent. Well, it is if we're being particularly kind.

COPPING AN EARFUL

Swordplay on wheels

Blimey! Talk about making life difficult for yourself. Below, Robert Citerne of France (left) is making a rapier thrust at Chong Zhang of China, in the World Wheelchair Fencing Championship in Turin. If there's any sport less suited to the wheelchair discipline, we'd like to hear about it. Anyone who says the pole vault gets a slap.

WHEELCHAIR FENCING

Six-legged piglet

Truly, these are great times for hideous freak animals – here we give you a pig with 150 per cent too many legs. Despite the fact that this six-legged piglet in Jiang Su Province, China, has an extra pair of legs getting in the way of its bum, it's still showing no signs of ill health and is growing up normally. Apparently, the weird wrinkly skin is normal.

HAM-STRUNG!

STAR WARS POSTBOX

The Postie strikes back

Personally, we don't much care what we put our letters into when we send them, as long as they get there – but in the USA, they have different ideas. This rather swish mailbox, which, as you can see, is designed to look like R2-D2 from the *Star Wars* films, stands on West 33rd Street in New York City, and we think it's rather cool. It would be even cooler if it projected holograms of Princess Leia when you put your letters in, but maybe that's asking for too much.

COLLECTION TIMES

STOP!

uspsjedimaster.com

For more weird stuff, go to...

NUTS.CO.UK/WEB

THE Nuts LIP

Rio Ferdinand: "At the World Cup, they had a big screen there, maybe they can take it off that corner of the stadium and put it over here..."

Man United vs Porto, 7:06pm United's defensive lynchpin gets bored sitting on the bench and decides to discuss that other hot topic: feng shui.

Alan Pardew: "F**k off, what are you pushing me back for?"
Arsene Wenger: "What do you want? What do you want? What do you want? You're a f**king disgrace!"

West Ham vs Arsenal, Upton Park, Sunday 5 November, 3.22pm West Ham score, Pardew celebrates and Wenger doesn't like it one bit.

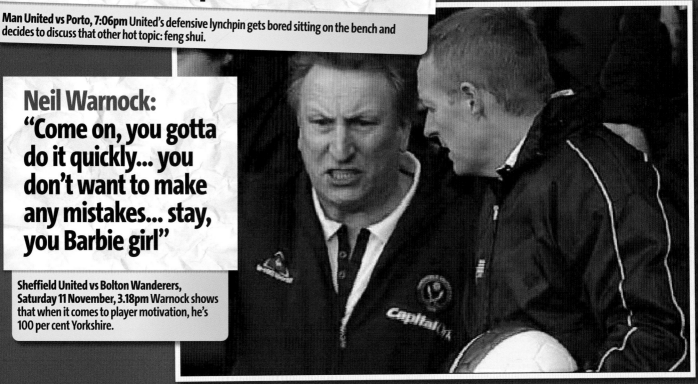

Neil Warnock: "Come on, you gotta do it quickly... you don't want to make any mistakes... stay, you Barbie girl"

Sheffield United vs Bolton Wanderers, Saturday 11 November, 3.18pm Warnock shows that when it comes to player motivation, he's 100 per cent Yorkshire.

READER!

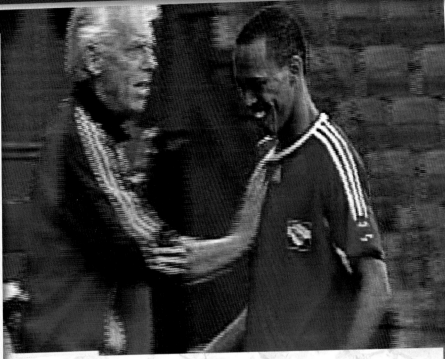

Leo Beenhakker: "Smile at me! Smile at me! Well done!"

Trinidad & Tobago vs Wales, Graz, 27 May, 6.47pm – The Trinidad coach insists substituted Densill Theobold doesn't leave the pitch until he smiles.

Aidy Boothroyd: "I don't really know. Ha-ha-ha! He's not very good!"

Watford vs Chelsea, Vicarage Road, Saturday 31 March, 5.34pm The Watford gaffer and Jose Mourinho share a laugh at the referee's incompetence.

Jose Mourinho: "Watch, he's going for you! Wants you outside, be careful!"

Chelsea vs Portsmouth, Saturday 21 October, 4.14pm – Mourinho warns Michael Ballack to be wary of yellow-card-happy referee Mark Clattenburg.

Shaun Wright-Phillips: "Hey, ref, hey! Have some f**king glasses on!"

Chelsea vs Liverpool, 4.35pm Little Shaun has a bit of trouble working out who's the referee and who's the referee's assistant.

Gerrard: "How did he get in there?"
Riise: "He just ran in there. It's not my fault"
Gerrard: "Don't tell me you didn't follow him"

Arsenal vs Liverpool, 5.44pm Gerrard and Riise blame each other for being crap as Gallas finishes off the Gooners' demolition of the Reds.

Cristiano Ronaldo: "You want this shirt? Do you want this? F**king hell!"

Man United vs Sheffield United, Old Trafford, Tuesday 17 April, 9.23pm The Reds' winger suggests to Chris Morgan they bring forward the post-match shirt-swapping.

Michael Owen: "Rooney's got sunglasses on front of his head"

Luton Airport, 5 June, 1.30pm – Owen's worried about Rooney's appearance as the players pose before boarding the plane to Germany.

Bloke busts finger playing football

"I ran in to tackle him, misjudged it, missed and crashed into the wall."

There's always one player in a football team who never stops, keeps on running when his team-mates have given up and who will do anything to win. In Scott Hudson's case, this meant careering into a wall after making a last-ditch challenge.

"We were drawing 0–0 and desperate not to lose as the game neared the end," the 28-year-old told us. "One of the opposition got the ball down the wing and looked threatening so I ran in to tackle him, misjudged it, missed and crashed into the wall. When I saw my finger, I was in shock. Luckily, it didn't hurt straight away, so I grabbed my mobile and took a few photos before the pain kicked in."

When Scott, a trainee driving instructor, arrived at A&E, they rushed him straight in before his dislocated finger went into spasm.

"The assisting nurse held my arm steady against my chest and the doc grabbed hold of my finger to snap it back into place," Scott remembers. "The pain was horrible, like he was trying to break the bone. But luckily, he managed to fix it first time."

Once Scott's finger was back to its normal state, the pain subsided, but he's still not happy: "The annoying thing is that I dislocated it two weeks ago and I still can't move it properly. It makes playing my PS2 really difficult!"

Uri Geller didn't take kindly to buses being late

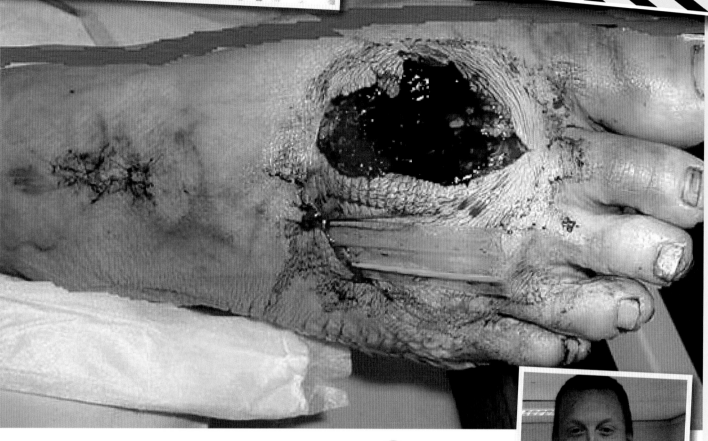

Car seat cuts foot

Nuts reader ruins foot in very nasty car smash

If you're queuing for a taxi in the cold and a mate pulls up to offer you a lift home, it's hard to say no. But when Nuts reader Scott Lowe from Aberdeen went along with his pals for a free ride, things took a turn for the worse.

"We'd been in the pub and were keen to get home," Scott tells us. "My mate knew the driver so I went along with them, but when he admitted it was his mum's car and he started speeding, I had second thoughts. Then he admitted he'd had a few drinks – just as he scraped along a line of parked cars, hit a traffic island at 80mph and flipped the car into a bus shelter."

The impact was so bad that Scott, 26, was knocked unconscious for ten minutes. The car was split in half and his supposed "mates" scarpered before the police arrived.

"When I came round, I was in an ambulance on the way to hospital and my foot was killing me because it'd got crushed under the car seat," he says.

"In total, I had ten different operations on my foot as it kept getting infected and the pins that were holding it together kept piercing the skin."

A year later, Scott still walks with a limp, but he's not bitter about the incident: "The lads at work call me 'peg leg', but I don't mind because I'm due a decent amount of compensation from the driver, which should make him think twice before driving like an idiot again."

Nuts TOP TENS

Richest players in hip-hop

The rap world's biggest bling merchants

1 P DIDDY – £172 MILLION
After selling his record label, Bad Boy Records, the cash has kept coming from Diddy's Sean John clothing line. His Unforgivable men's fragrance also averages sales of between $1.3 million and $1.5 million per week.

2 JAY-Z – £170 MILLION
The Jiggaman has got fingers in loads of pies that are bringing home the dough. From his stake in the New Jersey Nets basketball team and sales of Armadale vodka, to his 40/40 nightclubs and a salary as President of Def Jam records.

3 RUSSELL SIMMONS – £163 MILLION
The co-founder of Def Jam's never had a problem paying the bills thanks to his hugely successful media corporation, Rush Comms. Simmons recently launched his own credit card and still makes money from his Phat Farm fashion label.

4 DAMON DASH – £105 MILLION
The former co-founder of Roc-A-Fella records with Jay-Z has continued to do well for himself thanks to interests in Tiret Watches, America Magazine, New York nightclub The Plumm and even a boxing promotions company.

5 NEPTUNES – £78 MILLION
A recent survey revealed that the Neptunes produced almost 20 per cent of the tracks played on British radio and 43% of those played on American radio. That's a lot of royalty cheques.

6 DR DRE – £75 MILLION
The N.W.A. star is now a mega producer on his own label charging a generous "Friends and Family" rate of $75,000 per track for artists like Eminem and 50 Cent.

7 ICE CUBE – £71 MILLION
One of the original Gangsta Rappers has now moved from South Central L.A. to Hollywood where he is raking in the dosh as a leading man in the movies.

8 EMINEM – £55 MILLION
Slim Shady is now concentrating on producing and his own label Shady Records. If he doesn't take early retirement it's predicted that he'll become the richest rapper of all time.

=9 50 CENT – £50 MILLION
The Queens rapper hasn't wasted any time turning a profit since he burst on to the scene in 2003. His big money now comes from his own clothing line, a bottled water brand, video games and a booming acting career.

=9 NELLY – £50 MILLION
The St Louis rapper has made millions from clothing lines Vokal and Apple Bottoms as well as supplementing his income by being part owner of the Charlotte Bobcats NBA team with Michael Jordan.

I'm so rich I don't need to have a hat that fits.

SOURCES: THE PANACHE REPORT , US CENSUS BUREAU

Most crowded US states

#	State	Density
1	New Jersey	1,134.2 per sq mile
2	Rhode Island	1,003.2 per sq mile
3	Massachusetts	810 per sq mile
4	Connecticut	702.9 per sq mile
5	Maryland	541.8 per sq mile
6	New York	401.8 per sq mile
7	Delaware	400.8 per sq mile
8	Florida	296.3 per sq mile
9	Ohio	277.2 per sq mile
10	Pennsylvania	274 per sq mile

Biggest selling choc brands

The most-bought munchies beaters

1 **Dairy Milk** – 366,935 sold per week
2 **Galaxy** – 153,851 sold per week
3 **Maltesers** – 118,531 sold per week
4 **Mars** – 102,979 sold per week
5 **Quality Street** – 72,027 sold per week
6 **Aero** – 68,311 sold per week
7 **Roses** – 65,796 sold per week
8 **Celebrations** – 65,538 sold per week
9 **Kit Kat** – 62,569 sold per week
10 **Flake** – 61,542 sold per week

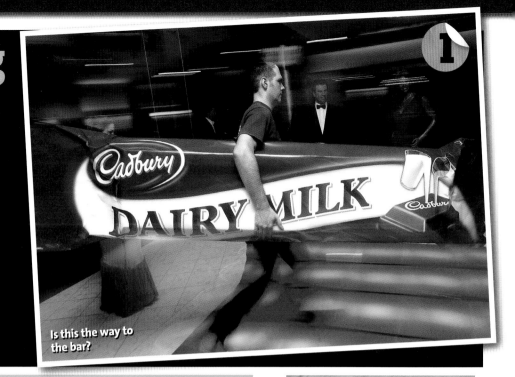

Is this the way to the bar?

Most murderous countries

Killings per 1000 population

1 **Colombia – 62**
2 South Africa – 50
3 **Jamaica – 32**
4 Venezuela – 32
5 **Russia – 20**
6 Mexico – 13
7 **Estonia – 11**
8 Latvia – 10
=9 **Lithuania – 10**
=9 Belarus – 10

SOURCES: THE GROCER, UNITED NATIONS, NASA, HOME OFFICE

Finding somewhere to live is murder in Medellin!

Fastest X-15 flights

America's fastest rocket plane pilots

1 **William Knight – 4,520mph**
2 William Knight – 4,261mph
3 **Joseph Walker – 4,105mph**
4 Robert White – 4,094mph
5 **Robert Rushworth – 4,018mph**
6 Neil Armstrong – 3,989mph
7 **John McKay – 3,938mph**
8 Robert Rushworth – 3,925mph
9 **Joseph Walker – 3,911mph**
10 William Dana – 3,910mph

WEV 297W

Most stolen cars in the uk

1 **Vauxhall Belmont – 436 stolen per 1000 registered**
2 Vauxhall Astra Mk2 – 376 stolen per 1000 registered
3 **Ford Escort Mk3 – 287 stolen per 1000 registered**
4 Austin/Morris Metro – 223 stolen per 1000 registered
5 **Vauxhall Nova – 207 stolen per 1000 registered**
6 Ford Orion – 167 stolen per 1000 registered
7 **Rover Metro – 134 stolen per 1000 registered**
8 Austin/Morris Maestro – 87 stolen per 1000 registered
9 **Austin/Morris Montego – 56 stolen per 1000 registered**
10 Ford Fiesta Mks1, 2 and 3 – 40 stolen per 1000 registered

The Best of Nuts
MESSAGE BOARDS

PEOPLE LOG ON AND LEAVE WEIRD AND WONDERFUL THINGS ON OUR MESSAGE BOARDS, MOSTLY PHOTOGRAPHS OF TOP WOMEN! HERE'S A SELECTION, AND DON'T FORGET TO LOG ON YOURSELF AT

WWW.NUTS.CO.UK

EMILY: "... here I am!""

Haylee's in her pants!

HAYLEE: "A new pic for you guys of moi!"

SAM: "It's bathtime!"

98

Clare's in the pink!

CLARE "This is my first pic – what do you think?"

KATY: "Hello everybody! I just thought I'd post a pic for you to check out!"

HANNAH: "This is me on my bed!"

BECKY: "Sexy new pic of my bum!"

KRINZIA: "Thought I'd share a piccy with you all!"

LAURA-JANE: "Thought I'd introduce myself – with this pic!"

THE TRUTH ABOUT WOMEN
WITH LUCY PINDER

NOT IN THE WORKPLACE
A girl at work has been giving me the eye and I fancy her. If I make a direct move I fear it may jeopardise my job. How do I get her away from the office?
Jamie, London

By just asking her for a drink after work! Mates do that all the time and it doesn't make it obvious that you fancy her – but if she's interested, she'll go. You can still make out you're just being friendly at first though.

CAN WE BE TOGETHER 3,000 MILES APART?
My girlfriend's been promoted at her work, but it involves moving to America. I can't ask her to turn it down, so what are your thoughts on a long-distance relationship?
Jason, Liverpool

Well, that's a very long distance relationship, isn't it? I personally wouldn't like it but the only thing you can do is try. I'll warn you right now, though, that it's going to be very difficult. Let it take its natural course but don't expect too much.

CAUGHT IN THE ACT
Me and my girlfriend were at it one night, when suddenly, her parents walked in on us. We

planned this big meal with them next week and I'm a bit nervous about it now, should I make an excuse or shall I put on a brave face and go?
Bob, Southampton

Don't make an excuse to miss it. You should just go because you've got to see them at some stage so that stage may as well be now. It's going to be really obvious why you're crying off if you do that, so get it done.

SHE'S A PORNO ADDICT
I originally introduced the idea of porn to my girlfriend early in our relationship but now she's obsessed and acts porno in a really lame way. How do I get her to move away from the idea?
Adam, Leeds

Again, I find myself saying this – be careful what you wish for! Leave your fantasies in the world of fantasy, or else you only have yourself to blame. If you got her into it, you can't very well then ask that she gets back out of it just like that. Just try and enjoy it as much as you can...

> ## "Leave your fantasies in the world of fantasy, or else you only have yourself to blame"

THE TRUTH ABOUT WOMEN WITH LUCY PINDER

DO I POP OFF TOO FAST?

I only last about five minutes when I'm with a lady. Does this mean I'm suffering from premature you-know-what?
Robert, London

That's fast! The fact is, though, that premature ejaculation is when you pop off in seconds, so you're not medically suffering from it. You just need to consider techniques that'll help you go at it for longer – the main one being to just slow down and stop thinking, "Oh, no! It's going to happen again!"

I DON'T LIKE HER GOING DOWN ON ME

Every time my girlfriend gives me oral attention, I feel bad – like I'm being degrading to her or something. Is this normal?
Ryan, Wigan

Put it this way Ryan, I don't think many blokes feel the same way you do! Think about it, your girlfriend wouldn't do it if she didn't enjoy it. Women can get a lot of pleasure out of giving pleasure. So, the next time she starts unzipping your jeans, try to sit back and remind yourself of that.

HE'S BIGGER THAN ME

I play five-a-side – and therefore shower – with my girlfriend's ex, so I've seen his wang and it's huge. I'm surely going to suffer by comparison, right?
Adam, Clapham

She left this bloke for a reason, Adam. Believe me, just because someone has a huge penis doesn't make them the boyfriend of the century. There are reasons why she split up with him and is now going

out with you, so I wouldn't worry. You are obviously doing something right. Plus, a lot of girls don't enjoy the massive ones.

SHOULD I BE MEAN?

I've been dating this girl for a few weeks now. She told me the other day to stop being so nice to her all the time, and to be horrible to her once in a while. What does she mean by this?
Sam, Gosport

Girls like guys who aren't a complete pushover, Sam. It can be unattractive if you let us get away with anything we want. It sounds to me like she wants you to put your foot down rather than just being "horrible" to her. So, don't start swearing at her – just don't be a lapdog!

MESSING WITH MY HEAD

I asked my best girl mate out but she said she wasn't interested in me in that way. Soon after, she put my hands on her breasts. She said she "just wanted a bit of attention" – what's she on about?
Jake, Manchester

She's just an attention-seeker, Jake. Full stop. I'd put all thoughts of romance with this girl right out of your head and make sure she doesn't behave like this again. Tell her, "Look, if you're not going to go out with me, you don't get any of the perks, OK?"

SHE'S BEEN AROUND!

I've just found out the girl I'm seeing has slept around a lot more than I have. Now I can't help worrying that I won't have the moves in the bedroom to keep her interested – any tips?
Stu, Croydon

Just try to put it right out of your mind, Stu. Seriously, she's not thinking about it, and it's not a competition to see who's better. If somebody is more experienced than you, it's easy to quickly get up to their "level" – look at it as a valuable learning curve.

MY MATES ARE ALL SETTLING DOWN

I'm 27 and my mates have all got long-term girlfriends, but I'm still happily single. I'm losing people to go out with! What can I do to stop it?
Adam, Buxton

Just try to encourage your mates to give you a bit of their time now and then, Adam. Make an active effort to entice them out. Don't their girlfriends have girls' night outs?

I CAN'T STOP BLUSHING AROUND WOMEN

Whenever I'm around girls I get really embarrassed. They can always see that I'm blushing – how can I make it stop?
Robert, Sunderland

"If somebody is more experienced than you, it's easy to quickly get up to their 'level' – look at it as a valuable learning curve"

If it really becomes a big problem for you, Robert, you can always give hypnosis a go. Have a look at www.bsch.org to find yourself a hypnotherapist. Otherwise, the best advice I can give is, before you approach a girl, just try to calm yourself down as much as you can. Bear in mind that there are a lot of girls out there who will find it very endearing and sweet, so don't stress yourself out unduly.

SHE'S USING HER WAD AGAINST ME

My girlfriend and I have always had a rocky relationship but just recently, she's come into a bit of money and every time we argue, she brings up all the stuff she's bought me. Now she's offered to pay for a holiday – what do I do?
Paul, Surrey

You have to address this with her, Paul, and say, "Look, I appreciate it when you buy me stuff but if you're going to use it as a weapon in an argument, I'd rather you didn't bother." It's not on and you have every right to tell her.

IS SHE FOR REAL?

How do I know if my girlfriend is faking it?
Stuart, Dunfermline

I've been asked this a few times, Stuart, and the answer is always that if she's good at faking it, you'll never know. Try not to worry about it – you might just be doing something right.

WAS I A DODGY SH*G?

I'd been going out with my girlfriend for about six weeks, but when I got her into bed for the first time and thought it went alright, she promptly dumped me the next morning. How can I get her back?
Liam, Cumbria

She doesn't sound like a very nice girl, Liam! If she's that quick to dismiss you for being, in her opinion, not very good in bed for just one night, then is she really worth trying to get back? I think not. She could have showed you a few things. To be honest, it sounds like she's not that into you, and not worth getting back.

WHY DO THEY WANT TO GET ME LAID?

I'm 19 and a virgin. My mates are pressuring me to have sex and it's really annoying. How do I get it through that I'm not interested?
Jamie, Milton Keynes

Boys will be boys, Jamie, but let them know it's annoying – if being a virgin doesn't bother you, why should it bother them? It's not their problem. Banter is fine, but if they're going on about it, they need to back off. I respect the fact that you're not too bothered about it – well done.

Twinned with the Orkney Islands town of Twatt?

DEAR NUTS,
I spotted this on a skiing holiday to Italy. Needless to say, I followed the sign.
Harry Neal, Birmingham
That Pussey looks rather cold, in our opinion.

It's pronounced "Vanker", honest

DEAR NUTS,
I saw this van on a recent lads' snowboarding trip to Austria. When I eventually stopped laughing I managed to get this picture and thought that it would be rude not to share it with you.
Stuart Coxhill, via email
Did you stick around and sing, "Who's the W*nker, who's the W*nker, who's the W*nker in the van?" at him?

I also have a brother named Dick

DEAR NUTS,
I came across a clip of this gentleman while I was surfing the Net. *surely* they are taking the p*ss?!
Paul, Co. Meath
The question is, what were you surfing the net for that led you to him?

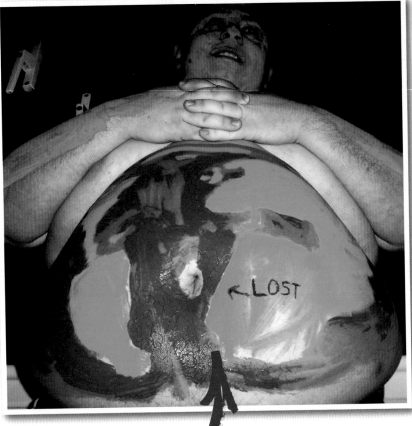

Welcome to Planet Girth

DEAR NUTS,
We were sitting in our flat bored so we decided to create our own globe on our flatmate's considerable belly. And after a while we thought that we could end everyone's misery and finally tell people where everyone on the *Lost* island is. It's actually my mate's belly button. Happy to clear that up.
Dale Howey, via email
You're clearly lying. The island in *Lost* is much smaller than your mate's belly button!

We didn't know they could do that!

DEAR NUTS,
This is me and my mate Mark in Spain. We thought you might like it…
Kenny Lee, Newmarket
Did you go inside to get a better taste of Quim's?

SHOW ME THE BUNNY

They hated Easter

SH*T HAPPENS

Banksy regretted having the beef madras

A DOG'S LIFE

"I'll get that damn cat back for this..."

MISTER MUSCLE

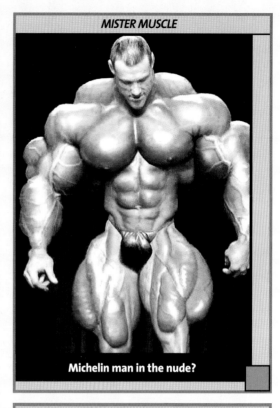

Michelin man in the nude?

LIBERTY TAKES A BREAK!

"Wish I lived in California..."

For more hilarious pictures, go to...

NUTS.CO.UK/WEB

Nuts CLUB STRIP CHALLENGE

LAURA
24, from Nottingham

Hi, Laura. Have you stripped in a nightclub before? No, this is my first time.

How about your boobs. Have they ever fallen out before? One time, I went commando, fell over and my dress came right up. And because it was so tight, I couldn't pull it down fast enough!

What's the best thing to do with your boobs? TThey're 30E, but I'm not really into my boobs in a sexual way. I'm more of a bum person.

What's the best way to give you an orgasm? Probably from behind. It turns me on because it turns the guy on.

Where's the strangest place you've done the business? On a washing machine in a launderette. The vibrations were very good!

What's the best way to chat you up? Some nice smiles and a bit of eye contact. Buy me a drink and no cheesy chat-up lines!

What chance do blokes like us have with a girl like you? So long as you're well-mannered, polite and well-spoken, you've got a pretty good chance.

Thanks to Aqua, Cardiff

DONNA
23, from Sevenoaks

Hi, Donna! Ever stripped in a club before? Yes. I was playing a drinking game. I'm rubbish at drinking games so I lost and ended up extremely naked.

What's the best way to chat you up? Buy me lots of drinks and tell me I've got lovely eyes and a nice bum.

Ever kissed a girl? Yes, but only a peck on the lips. I've never snogged a girl properly. But I'll tell you who I'd love to snog – Christina Aguilera.

Ever had sex in the toilets? Yes, on holiday in Turkey. It wasn't meant to happen but we got carried away.

Ever thrown up over someone you fancy? Yes! I was drunk and I threw up over his shoes. I'd snogged him at the beginning of the evening but funnily enough, I didn't snog him again after that.

Sexual fantasy? Two women. And me!

What will your friends think when they see you in *Nuts*?
I'll probably get loads of stick for it, especially as I'm stripping.

Thanks to bykerbabe.com

NutsJOKES

DIY or face the consequences

A wife, frustrated by her husband's bone-idleness around the house in the DIY department, sees cause for concern one day when the toilet clogs up. She decides to ask if he'd mind seeing to it, and is greeted with a gruff, "What do I look like, a toilet cleaner?"

The next day the waste disposal unit seizes up. Summoning all her courage she says, "Sorry to bother you, dear. The waste disposal's broken – would you try to fix it for me?"

"Who do I look like? Some sort of plumber?

Get me a beer and sod off!" he replies.

To cap it all, the next day the washing machine goes on the blink and, taking her life in her hands, the wife addresses the sofa-bound slob: "Darling, I know you're busy, but the washing machine's packed up."

"Oh, and I suppose I look like a bl**dy washing machine repairman?" her old man says.

Finally fed up, she calls out three different repairmen to come and fix her appliances.

That evening, she informs her husband of

this. He frowns angrily and asks, "So how much will it cost?"

"Well, they said I could pay them either by baking a cake or having sex," she says.

"What type of cakes did you bake?" he growls.

"Who do I look like, Delia Smith?" she replies.

She can't step up

One day at a bus stop there's a girl wearing a skintight miniskirt.

Just as she's about to get on the bus she realises that her skirt is so tight she can't lift her foot high enough to reach the first step.

Thinking it will give her enough slack to raise her leg, she reaches back and unzips her skirt a little. However, she can't reach the step, so she reaches back once again to unzip it a little more. But still she can't reach the step.

So, with her skirt zipper halfway down, she reaches back and unzips it all the way. Thinking that she can get on the step now, she lifts up her leg only to realize it's still impossible.

Seeing how embarrassed the girl is, the man standing behind her puts his hands around her waist and lifts her up on to the first step of the bus. The girl turns around furiously and screams, "How dare you touch my body that way, I don't even know you!"

Shocked, the man says, "Well, after you reached around and unzipped my fly three times, I figured that we were friends."

"We're all going on a Summer Holiday"

Trial and error

Tried in a hostile town, a man doesn't think he has a chance of getting off a murder charge. So, shortly before the jury retires he bribes one of the jurors to find him guilty of the lesser crime of manslaughter.

The jury is out for over three days before eventually returning a verdict of manslaughter.

The relieved defendant collars the bribed juror and says: "Thanks. How ever did you manage it?"

"It wasn't easy," admits the juror. "All the others wanted to acquit you."

Q: How do you know if there is a fighter pilot at a party?
A: He'll tell you

Male persuasion

Little Johnny walks past his parents room one night and sees them making love. Puzzled, he asks his father about it the next morning. "Why were you doing that to mummy last night?"

His father replies, "Because mummy wants a baby."

The next night, Johnny spots mummy giving daddy a blowjob and the next morning he asks his father, "Why was mummy doing that to you last night?"

His father replies, "Because mummy wants a BMW."

Q: What will history remember Bill Clinton as?
A: The President after Bush

Ex-pletive FM

A competition is running on a local radio station.

"Right," says the DJ. "If you can think of a word in normal every day use that is not in the dictionary then you win £100."

Only one light comes on the phone banks and the DJ punches it quickly.

"Hi, caller. What's your word?" says the DJ.

"GOAN," says the caller.

"How do you spell that?" says the DJ.

"G-O-A-N," the caller replies.

"Well, that's certainly not in the dictionary but before you get the money can you tell me how you would use it in a sentence?"

"Goan F**k yoursel..." the caller says.

The DJ cuts him off and apologises to his audience for the bad language. Thankfully, another call comes in and the DJ is relieved to be able to move on.

"What's your word, caller?" he enquires.

"SMEE," says the caller.

"And how do you spell that?" asks the DJ.

"S-M-E-E," says the caller.

"Well, you're correct, SMEE isn't in the dictionary," says the DJ, "But before we give you the money can you tell me how you would use that in a sentence?"

"Smee again," says the caller. "Now Goan F**k yourself."

Hard cell

It's a stockbroker's first day in prison and his psychotic-looking cell mate notices how scared the stockbroker looks and decides to put him at ease.

"I'm in for a white-collar crime, too" he says.

"Oh, really?" says the stockbroker, sighing with relief.

"Yes," says the cellmate, "I killed a vicar."

"Any chance of a lift, mate?"

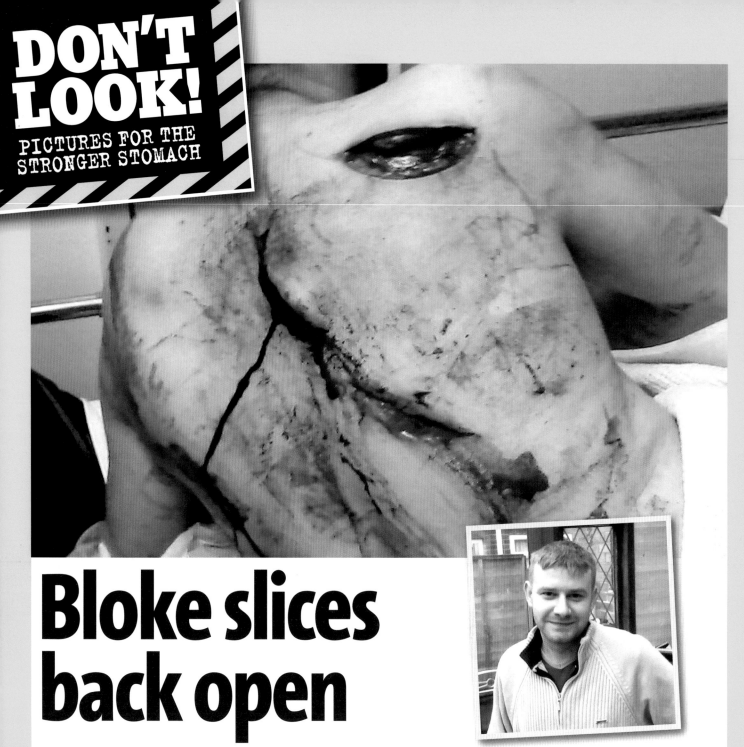

Bloke slices back open

"I clambered out of the loft window... then everything went wrong"

We're always told that smoking is bad for your health. Well, here's all the proof you need in the shape of *Nuts* reader Gareth Skinn, who sliced his back open when he smoked a cigarette out of his attic window.

"I'd been on a stag do with my mates and was a little worse for wear," the 23-year-old tells us. "I popped up to my attic bedroom for a quick ciggie but, just as the nicotine rush hit me, I dropped the bl**dy thing out the window. When I looked down, I could see it was within arm's reach, so I clambered out to retrieve it. Then everything went wrong."

He slipped and crashed – back first – straight through his parents' conservatory roof. He was knocked out and the broken plastic sliced his back open.

"When I came round, my brother and his mates were stood around me. There was blood everywhere and I was lying naked on the floor. Luck- ily, they rushed me straight to hospital where the doctors went to work and put 16 stitches in me. I was let out the same night and was off work for a couple of weeks. Now when I smoke out of the attic window, if I drop my ciggie I just spark up a fresh one. I don't think my mum would forgive me if I wrecked her conservatory for a second time!"

READTH
ISWHILE
ICHECK
OUTYOU
RTITS

Mirror-punching mistake

"Dad picked up my knuckle and I thought, 'This is bad!'"

There's not a man alive who hasn't got carried away in front of the mirror and started throwing a few punches. Survivor's *Eye Of The Tiger* gets louder in your head and, before you know it, you're yelling, "Adrian!" at the top of your voice, thrusting your fist into the air in triumph. Or, in the case of *Nuts* reader Brett Shepherd, 17, accidentally putting your fist through said mirror, cutting short your career as a pugilist.

"I was shadow-boxing in my room," Essex lad Brett tells us, "but I mistimed one of the punches, put my fist through the mirror and a massive hole in the wall.

"It was almost like a scene from a gory horror film. My hand was knackered, blood was spraying everywhere and I thought: 'F**k me, this is bad!' I stuck it under the tap in the kitchen sink and my dad picked up what he thought was a bit of skin. It turned out to be a piece of knuckle that I'd sliced off. That's when I knew I needed to go to hospital."

Once there, hospital staff told Brett that he had, in fact, sliced the top off his knuckle and severed three tendons, so he needed plastic surgery and major physiotherapy.

"When I came round from the general anaesthetic, I had over 50 stitches in my hand, which they then put in a cast," adds Brett. "I only did it two weeks ago and I have to do physio every day, but the best thing is that I'm off work for three months, and playing games on my PlayStation all day counts as physio. Result!"

Nuts PUB AMMO

Sky Sports' new 'eagle cam' raised eyebrows

✳ The Wembley arch is 133 metres high

✳ **The most popular civilian car in Iraq is the Toyota Corolla.**
✳ No Stockinger-made safe has ever been broken into in the company's 30-year history.

✳ **1.09 billion people use the internet every day.**
✳ There are 4,360 known species of frog.
✳ **A hand grenade measures 0.5 on the Richter scale, the Nagasaki atom bomb 5.**
✳ The English Civil War was the biggest military mobilization in English history.
✳ **Mars has two moons.**
✳ **MC Hammer**'s *Please Hammer Don't Hurt 'Em* was the first hip-hop album to sell 10 million copies.

✳ **The steam engine was invented in ancient Greece.**
✳ **Chicken Tikka Masala** was invented in Glasgow.
✳ **Ernie Els has scored an eagle in the Masters every year since 2002.**

✳ Ten-pin bowling was first shown on television in 1947.
✳ **Einstein published his theory of relativity in 1905.**
✳ Only 13 soldiers in Denmark's army were killed during the German invasion in WWII.
✳ **There are 11 time zones in Russia.**
✳ The smallest written version of the New Testament is 1/5 inch thick.
✳ **George Bush has fallen off his bike three times in the last three years.**
✳ A species of slime-mold beetle has been named after former U.S. Defence Secretary Donald Rumsfeld.
✳ **There is a 400 sq km chamber of molten magma 10km beneath the crust of the Vesuvius volcano.**
✳ One day on Venus is 5,832 hours long — the equivalent to 243 days on Earth.
✳ **20 million tropical fish go from the sea into aquariums in Europe and the US every year.**
✳ Light travels at 670.6 mph.
✳ **David Jones is the most common male name in the UK.**
✳ The May Day stadium in North Korea has a floor area of 207,000 square metres.
✳ The largest recorded crocodile

✳ **Pablo Picasso painted 20,000 artworks in his lifetime.**

Can the last person to bed turn the lights out?

✳ **36 million people live in the Greater Tokyo area ...**

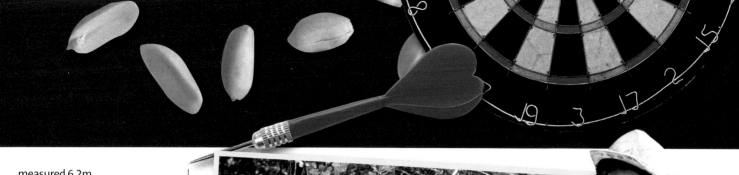

measured 6.2m.

✳ **Brits take 2.8 million cans of baked beans on holiday every year.**

✳ Space begins at an altitude of 62 miles.

✳ **Leeds United's Elland Road has the biggest capacity for any club outside the Premiership.**

✳ The harmonica is the world's best-selling musical instrument.

✳ **Ninety-two nuclear bombs have been lost at sea.**

✳ The South American giant anteater eats more than 30,000 ants a day.

✳ **There are 1,040 islands around Britain, one of which is the smallest island in the world: Bishop's Rock.**

At full throttle, a chainsaw blade can reach 45mph.

He always went overboard when cutting the beef

Thank god I shaved my underarms

✳ **The first Miss World competition was held in 1951**

✳ Korfball is the only sport played with mixed teams, consisting of four men and four women.

✳ **The last man to be hanged in the UK was called Peter Anthony Allen.**

✳ If a human ran at the top speed of a Cheetah the 100m world record would fall to three seconds.

✳ **Manchester Utd have been taking part in European competitions for 50 years.**

✳ It's been nine years since the FA Cup holders were last knocked out at the third round.

✳ **One 8x4x4-inch lump of lumber can make 4.4 million postage stamps.**

✳ **Silver can sterilise water.**

✳ Will Smith holds the world record for attending film premieres – three in 12 hours for *Hitch*.

✳ **A sloth's top speed is 1mph.**

✳ Diamonds are brought up to the Earth's surface in volcanic explosions.

✳ **There are 20 UFO sightings filed with the National UFO Reporting Centre in the US every day.**

✳ Fantasy sports players spend on average 3.8 hours a week managing their team.

✳ **The first appendectomy was performed on board a submarine in WWII.**

✳ During Vietnam 76 per cent of wounded soldiers survived.

✳ **The required length of a banana under EU rules is 14cm.**

✳ 80 per cent of France's electricity is generated by nuclear power.

✳ **A T Rex skeleton was sold to Chicago's Field Museum in 1997 for $8.4 million.**

✳ The World Record for the highest stunt fall into a mattress is 232 feet.

✳ **The longest non-stop Space Invaders marathon lasted 38 hours and 37minutes.**

Maserati MC12 Edo Competition XX

Based on the Ferrari Enzo, the standard Maserati MC12 puts out an incredible 624bhp. This Edo Competition XX tuned version produces 800bhp at 8,500rpm – an increase in power of 176bhp!

- The V12 6.3-litre engine has new camshafts and conrods that ramp the power up to the 800bhp mark – which is about the same power output as you'll get from a modern Formula One car!
- This version is also 100kg lighter than the standard car.
- 0–60mph comes up in under 3.2 secs, with a top speed of 244mph!
- The tailpipes are made from ultra-lightweight carbon fibre.
- A trick tyre air-pressure monitor displays the pressure and temperature for each tyre.
- The Edo Competition XX has independent and fully adjustable suspension.

Buy the car with the "Edo" kit and you get one day's testing with an instructor plus mechanics and data recording.

- A standard Maserati MC12 costs £520,000 – expect to pay £70,000 more for this monster.

LADIES CONFESS
TO OUR SECRETARY

"I was driven wild by three girls"

My friends and I had kissed a few times and had a little grope before. We love blokes but were curious to explore. They asked me over one night to join in some fun and I agreed. After a few bottles of wine, the conversation turned horny. A few of the girls showed us naughty positions, one acted out oral sex on a banana and before I knew it, clothes started coming off. My friend pushed me down on the bed and unbuttoned my top. Another kissed my nipples and I groaned out loud. As I laid back, I felt hands between my thighs. Fingers dived in and out of me and I was being driven wild by three gorgeous girls. We took turns on each other and explored lots of angles. Although most of us have fellas, we still try to meet up once a month for a "girls' night in"!
Natalie, Manchester

"I got wet just watching them"

I'd just had a flat-warming party and two of my new neighbours – a young couple – stayed for a nightcap after everyone had left. He was a very fit bloke and she was a gorgeous blonde. They'd been getting frisky with each other all night, and I felt the same. As the drink started flowing, the three of us started flirting with each other. I decided to get another drink but when I returned, she was sucking hard on his enormous manhood. I was getting so wet just watching them, I slid my hand into my knickers and started moaning with pleasure. The guy heard me and started focusing on me as I rubbed myself, staring back at him as I writhed in a state of ecstasy. It felt so dangerous that the girl had no idea I was pleasuring myself behind her, but that made the orgasm more intense, and me and the guy both came together. As he filled his girlfriend's mouth, I sneaked off, then returned pretending to be innocent and unaware. I love it when they come round now!
Natasha, Manchester

"Our clothes came off in seconds"

Last summer, I went to work at a summer camp in New York. As soon as I got there, I started to flirt outrageously with one of my male colleagues. His name was Heath and he was gorgeous, but that's all I knew about him. One night, we snuck off to his private cabin and, as soon as the door was shut, we got right down to it. Our clothes were off in seconds and the sex was hard and fast. He then laid me down and took me from behind. I have to admit, it was the best sex I'd ever had, and I came in no time. That night was definitely the highlight of my summer.
Pamela, Belfast

"We went for it hard and fast"

My friend and I won some tickets to a music-awards party on a radio show, and were so excited when we got there and saw all the celebs. After a few hours, I was on a high from all the free champagne and was feeling naughty. I saw the sexy lead singer of a popular band and, feeling confident in my slinky outfit, followed him into the bathroom. He pulled me into one of the cubicles and gave me the most passionate kiss as he ran his rough hands all over my writhing body. I took him in my mouth and worked on him for a while, before he pulled me up and took me against the toilet door. The sex was so hot, we both came instantly. My friend still doesn't believe me!
Danni, Essex

"He slowly took off my trousers"

One Sunday afternoon, my boyfriend and I were at his place having a lazy day in bed. We were

"I came almost straight away"

I hadn't seen my boyfriend for a while and we were pent up with sexual frustration. Within seconds of meeting, we were at it on the couch. We wanted more than a quick fumble so we got into bed, our hands groping at each other. I came almost straight away from just his fingers and then he moved down further and started licking me. He couldn't believe how wet I was, which turned us on even more. I had another amazing orgasm and, as I was catching my breath, he came all over my breasts. I fell asleep in his arms but woke up in the early hours. I felt horny again and started touching myself while he slept. Knowing he could wake up and catch me turned me on. I soon climaxed, stifling my groans of pleasure and lay there smiling cheekily as he lay there with no idea what had just happened.
Jade, Staffs

watching a film but also feeling very horny. He started to touch me, rubbing me all over. I couldn't resist, so I turned around and we started kissing passionately. He slowly took off my trousers and thong and rubbed me while I played with his manhood. He gently parted my legs and slid his shaft deep into me from behind, making me moan and want him more. After five minutes, my boyfriend was so turned on he begged me to ride him. Hearing him say this made me moan even more. I told him to take me to the shower, where he bent me over and slipped deep inside me. It was amazing with the hot steaming water and the passion between us. I can't wait until our next lazy afternoon!
Nikki, Leeds

"I climbed on top of him"

My boyfriend and I went on a drive one evening but ended up in a supermarket car park feeling really horny. We started to kiss and my boyfriend reached over and slid his hand between my legs. I was getting really turned on and started playing with myself while he watched. The excitement was too much for him and he undid his trousers and began to pleasure himself, too. We were both so close to coming, but I needed to feel him inside me. There were still quite a few people around in the car park but we just had to have each other, so I climbed up on top of him and we had fantastic sex on the front seat of his car until we both had the most intense orgasms ever! Definitely the best trip to a supermarket I've ever had!
Nicki, Midlands

"We were naked on the bus"

I was on the way back from work and caught my usual number 14 bus and went upstairs, passing an old lady who was at the bottom of the stairs. To my excitement, there was this hot, tanned guy sitting alone who I'd noticed a few times before. I walked towards him but the bus jolted forward and I fell on top of him. I seized the opportunity and undid his jeans. Suddenly, we were caught up in a fit of passion. He sucked my breasts while I felt his bulging package. I had just climbed on top of him when the old lady must have come up and seen us. She must have raised the alarm as the bus abruptly stopped. We quickly ran off. I saw the guy on the same bus the next day and he gave me a cheeky grin that showed he wanted to finish what we'd begun!
Katie, Southampton

"He explored me with his tongue"

Last Saint Patrick's Day, I was stewarding on a float for the Fire Brigade. I was wearing a really revealing female leprechaun outfit and saw a sexy fireman. I was becoming more and more turned on as the day went by. I went to the back of the truck only to find myself face-to-face with the gorgeous fireman. We ended up kissing passionately before he explored me with his tongue and gradually we abandoned our clothes – except for his fireman's hat and my leprechaun's hat! He gently parted my legs and I moaned with ecstasy as he slipped inside me and I climaxed immediately. I then took him in my mouth until he came. It was the sexiest situation I've ever been in, surrounded by thousands of people. When the truck stopped, we emerged with our clothes on and without anybody knowing our little secret.
Shauna, Ireland

"She slowly unzipped my jeans"

My girlfriend and I were on the train to her house. It was a really long journey and I was bored, so I decided to go for a sleep. While I was still kind of awake, I could feel something rubbing up and down my thigh. I opened my eyes a little and my girlfriend looked at me and gave me a kiss, while she gently rubbed her hands over my groin. She started kissing my neck until I was really horny and really wet. Then, she slowly unzipped my jeans and moved her fingers inside me and gave me the best orgasm I've ever had. I found it so impossibly hard not to be really loud, especially because I came so hard. Now, we try to do it in every new place we can.
Kirsty, Bedfordshire

"I climaxed second in the changing room"

I'd just returned from a holiday without my boyfriend so when we saw each other again, we were both really horny. We decided to go swimming at a local hotel. We messed about in the pool kissing and touching each other, which got us really turned on. We then sneaked back into the blokes' changing rooms and before I knew it, he slipped his hands down my bikini bottoms where I was already very wet. Gasping, we closed the door and I climbed on top of him. The excitement of where we were and the fact we could have been caught at any minute meant we both climaxed in seconds. It was definitely the sexiest changing room I've ever been in!
Victoria, Blackpool

Most expensive cars on the planet

1 BUGATTI VEYRON – £840,000
A deposit of £220,000 will secure you this 252mph monster. Only 16 Veyrons have been sold in the UK out of a total production run of 300, making the world's most expensive motor an instant collectors' item.

2 MASERATI MC12 VERSIONE CORSE – £676,000
No surprise that this 755bhp beast is also on *Nuts'* fantasy shopping list. It may cost an arm, a leg and a head but only 12 will be made and the price tag includes exclusive invitations to Maserati events worldwide.

3 PAGANI ZONDA F ROADSTER – £450,000
The only way this car could look meaner is with the bare carbon fibre bodywork finish from the options list, and that'll set you back an extra £112,500.

4 KOENIGSEGG CCX – £370,000
For the price of a Veyron you could buy two of these and still have £100,000 left over in loose change. Maybe you should spend that on the carbon fibre wheels or ceramic brakes – neither of which are standard.

5 BRISTOL FIGHTER T – £352,000
Powered by twin turbochargers this Westcountry slugger is an aerodynamic masterpiece that hardly makes a dent in the wind tunnel. It will make a considerable dent on your wallet, though. .

=6 MERCEDES SLR McLAREN – £340,000
A jet fighter on wheels. Or a jet fighter on polished-rim lightweight alloys to be more precise. For the price of a 208mph SLR you could buy a fleet of 22 brand new Seat Ibiza's. Your choice.

=6 MAYBACH 62 S – £340,000
Mercedes made sure its Rolls-Royce rival was longer, faster and more luxurious than anything on the market. This is the limo of choice for Presidents and Russian Mafiosi because it can make it from 0-62mph in 5.2 seconds.

8 SALEEEN S7 – £300,000
From the company that usually makes rednecks' dreams come true, by modifying their pick-ups, comes a 200mph supercar. The S7 will get you from 0-100mph and back again in 11.2 seconds.

9 ROLLS-ROYCE PHANTOM – £250,000
Like a penthouse suite on wheels this is the seventh incarnation of the Phantom that dates back to 1925. But we bet that one didn't have umbrellas that pop out of the rear doors.

10 ASCARI KZ1 – £235,000
Only 50 of these 5.0 litre V8 dream machines will ever be built. Included in the price: your very own racetrack in Southern Spain where you can tool around with the 49 other KZ1 owners.

Premiership away dayers
Fans that travel 1000+ miles a year

=1	Portsmouth	45%
=1	Middlesbrough	45%
3	Sheffield Utd	41%
4	Chelsea	36%
5	Man Utd	30%
=6	Watford	27%
=6	Newcastle	27%
=8	Bolton	26%
=8	Spurs	26%
10	West Ham	25%

Are we there yet?

Oldest Popes
More sanatogen, your holiness?

1	Leo XIII	93
2	Clement XII	87
3	Clement X	86
=4	Pius IX	85
=4	Innocent XII	85
6	John Paul II	84
=7	Gregory XIII	83
=7	Paul IV	83
=7	Benedict XIV	83
=7	Pius VII	83

SOURCES: MSN, NEXIS, VIRGIN MONEY

Coldest years in the UK

1. **1740 – 6.86** *degrees centigrade average (dca)*
2. 1695 – 7.29 dca
3. **1879 – 7.44 dca**
=4. 1694 – 7.67 dca
=4. **1698 – 7.67 dca**
6. 1692 – 7.73 dca
7. **1814 – 7.78 dca**
8. 1784 – 7.85 dca
9. **1688 – 7.86 dca**
10. 1675 – 7.88 dca

Brrr, I've got snow balls

UK'S most popular crisps

1. **Walker's – 381,345 bags sold per week**
2. **Pringles – 121,276 bags sold per week**
3. **Sensations – 86,107 bags sold per week**
4. **McCoy's – 77,648 bags sold per week**
5. **Doritos – 68,549 bags sold per week**
6. **Quavers – 64, 568 bags sold per week**
7. **Hula Hoops – 56,672 bags sold per week**
8. **Mini Cheddars – 42,436 bags sold per week**
9. **Wotsits – 40,517 bags sold per week**
10. **KP – 32,783 bags sold per week**

Emptiest US States

1. **Wyoming – 493,782**
2. Vermont – 608,827
3. **Alaska – 626,932**
4. North Dakota – 642,200
5. **South Dakota – 754,844**
6. Delaware – 783,600
7. **Montana – 902,195**
8. Rhode Island – 1,048,319
9. **Hawaii – 1,211,537**
10. New Hampshire – 1,235,786

Ugliest sports stars

1. **Wayne Rooney – 679 votes**
2. Peter Beardsley – 676 votes
3. **Ronaldinho – 507 votes**
4. Peter Crouch – 490 votes
5. **Ricky Hatton – 410 votes**
6. Boris Becker – 388 votes
7. **Paul Gascoigne – 285 votes**
8. Luke Chadwick – 211 votes
9. **Prince Naseem – 187 votes**
10. Martin Keown – 167 votes

Prison populations in Europe

The world's most stacked slammers

1. **Germany – 80,413 prisoners**
2. **England/Wales – 76,678 prisoners**
3. **Spain – 61,333 prisoners**
4. Italy – 56,530 prisoners
5. **France – 52,908 prisoners**
6. Netherlands – 20,747 prisoners
7. **Portugal – 13,034 prisoners**
8. Belgium – 9,245 prisoners
9. **Austria – 8,883 prisoners**
10. Sweden – 7,054 prisoners

Colditz anyone? All German prisons look the same.

Most successful Cricket World Cup teams

1. **Australia – 51 wins**
2. England – 36
=3. **West Indies – 35**
=3. New Zealand – 35
5. **India – 32**
6. Pakistan – 30
7. **South Africa – 26**
8. Sri Lanka – 25
9. **Zimbabwe – 8**
10. Kenya – 6

SOURCE: THE MET OFFICE, US CENSUS BUREAU, ONEPOLL, THE GROCER, INTERNATIONAL CENTRE FOR PRISON STUDIES, CRICINFO

GIRLS IN THE SHOWER

They're wet, topless and soapy – how much more of an introduction do you need?